Praise for *Your Money and Your Mind*

"Gosh, this is an important book! We know deep down that money impacts our sense of wellbeing, but it's sometimes hard to put our finger on why that is the case, let alone what to do about it. In this excellent book, Adam draws on years of research, in-the-trenches work as a financial planner and from his own experience to offer practical explanations and suggestions to balance our money and our minds. There is life-changing information here – read it, digest it and be free!"

—Pete Matthew, author, *The Meaningful Money Handbook* and chief executive officer, Jacksons Wealth Management

"Adam Cockerham is my financial adviser and is helping me prepare for retirement, but this book is not a pitch for products or tactics. It is something better. It is an invitation to think more clearly about money, work, security and the passing of time. Drawing on Stoicism, Buddhism and Western thought, Adam reminds us that money is a tool, not a verdict on our worth, and that clarity of thought and peace of mind are among the most undervalued assets of all.

"Adam understands markets, risk and planning, but he also understands people. That combination is rare. If you are approaching a moment of change in life or thinking about retirement, this book offers a deep understanding of what truly matters and how to invest wisely in order to enjoy it."

—Lord Thomas Watson, Baron Watson of Wyre Forest

"Our experience of money is deeply interwoven into the structure of our lives – impacting on the material world, our psychology, sense of self and wellbeing. Our relationship to money is often surprisingly visceral, touching something deeper in us than we might expect. It can bring up questions of self-worth, shame, power, personal security, and tension both within ourselves and in our relationships.

"What Adam does so well in this book is meet these experiences head on. He explores our relationship with money through a thoughtful blend of psychological insight and philosophical reflection, while keeping the ideas grounded and relatable. Importantly, he doesn't stop at insight – he offers clear, practical guidance on what to do when these challenges arise in everyday life.

"This is a book that works both as a coherent whole and as a resource to return to when specific issues emerge. It invites reflection while equipping the reader with tools for meaningful change."

—Jonathan Armes, chartered occupational psychologist

"It's rare to find someone who truly understands markets, planning, and the human mind. That combination is powerful, and you feel it on every page of *Your Money and Your Mind*. Adam doesn't give you tactics. He gives you clarity, the kind that changes how you think, feel, and act around money.

"If money has ever taken up more space in your head than it should, read this book. It might just give you your mind back."

—Abraham Okusanya, founder and
chief executive officer, Timeline

"'I replaced my empty pursuit of hedonism with an almost obsessive pursuit of external validation.' Adam Cockerham's confession in the preface resonates strongly. When we believe a certain goal guarantees the happiness we deserve, only to feel empty upon achieving it, the problem isn't the goal or the pursuit; it's our mindset. In this book, Adam unpicks the tangled webs we weave around us as we go through life, to help us understand what the ancients already knew: money is not the 'root of all evil'; rather, the love of money is. When we learn to put money in its rightful place in our lives, we are free from its anxious influence. Only then can we use it for the right purposes, for ourselves and for others, while enjoying the true prosperity of inner peace."

—Simoney Kyriakou, editor, FTAdviser

"I think about money a lot. As the CEO of a nature finance company, I've spent the last decade trying to build a bridge between people's relationship with money and the recovery of Earth's ecosystems. It's work that forces you to confront an uncomfortable truth: the same psychological patterns that drive overconsumption and financial anxiety are the ones degrading the natural world. Adam arrives at this truth from a completely different starting point. He elegantly explores ancient philosophy, psychology, and a decade of working with real people, making real decisions about their money.

"What strikes me is that he's working on the same problem from the opposite direction. Where I'm trying to fix humanity's relationship with the planet through money, Adam is trying to fix our relationship with money through the mind. Both require the same thing: seeing clearly, letting go of the stories we tell ourselves, and understanding that real wealth, ecological or financial, is something we already have if we stop long enough to notice it.

"This book won't tell you where to invest. It will make you a better investor in your own life and help you become more grounded in things that add true value to you. Perhaps, it will also help you become a better steward of the world around you."

—Cain Blythe, founder and chief executive officer, Creditnature and Ecosulis

"Long-term savings and investment markets are driven by a mix of technical inputs and sentiment. This complex mix cascades down to us all as individuals. Adam Cockerham places himself right at the intersection between the two and provides a fresh perspective on what is really at play within the individual and what ultimately shapes our sense of financial wellbeing. In a world that is rapidly transitioning to the AI era, this book provides a timely reminder that technical prowess alone is not a guarantee for our overall peace of mind. This thought-provoking book is as relevant to the professional adviser as it is to the client."

—Phillip Howell, chairman, The Openwork Partnership

"Adam and his book have dared to bridge the gap between the everyday provision of financial advice (which anyone can get if they look hard enough and in the right place – an ongoing challenge for our industry!) and holistic financial coaching. The fundamental difference is understanding what people really want to achieve in their lives and beyond – their hopes, dreams and aspirations for themselves and sometimes, the next generation – and how people rationalise their thoughts about their finances.

In doing so, financial planners can help their clients to reframe their inherent biases and enable them to make clearer decisions about their money.

"Adam has expertly navigated this subject by blending ancient teachings with current psychology and he has highlighted the impact through some of his own personal financial planning interactions. This approach can truly make a difference to peoples' lives, not because following the principles of this book will make its readers wealthier but because they will have a clearer mind when making decisions about their money and feel better about what their financial plan will deliver for them."

—Stuart Dodson, chief executive officer,
True Potential Wealth Management

Your Money and Your Mind

Your Money and Your Mind

Discover the *Real* Route to Financial Freedom

Adam Cockerham

HARRIMAN HOUSE
www.harriman-house.com

First published in 2026 by Harriman House, an imprint of Pan Macmillan
EU Representative: Macmillan Publishers Ireland Ltd, 1st Floor, The Liffey Trust Centre, 117-126 Sheriff Street Upper, Dublin 1, D01 YC43
Associated companies throughout the world
www.panmacmillan.com

Paperback ISBN: 978-1-80409-357-3
eBook ISBN: 978-1-80409-358-0

British Library Cataloguing in Publication Data
A CIP catalogue record for this book can be obtained from the British Library.

01 Printed and bound by CPI Group (UK) Ltd.

Cover Design by Heat Design.

Contents

Disclaimer

THIS BOOK IS intended for informational and educational purposes only. The views expressed are those of the author and do not constitute financial advice tailored to individual circumstances. Readers are encouraged to seek professional financial advice before making any financial decisions.

This book contains personal reflections on mental health, well-being and spirituality. It is not a substitute for professional medical, psychological or therapeutic advice. If you are experiencing mental health challenges, please consult a qualified health professional.

The author and publisher disclaim any liability for any loss or risk, personal or otherwise, incurred as a consequence of the information contained in this book.

Foreword

IN A WORLD that often feels chaotic, unpredictable and driven by forces beyond our control, the search for clarity and understanding seems incredibly important. All areas of life that come into view in our day-to-day experience – financial, personal, work and societal – leave us with a tangled web of beliefs, assumptions and deeply ingrained habits of thought. In this book, Adam Cockerham skilfully unpacks these complexities, weaving together deep insights into how the mind works with a nuanced exploration of money, value and the forces that shape our perception of wealth and what we call success.

I have had the privilege of working with Adam for some three years and he has been a superb student of THOUGHT INTELLIGENCE®, exhibiting a profound yet elegantly simple understanding of how our minds shape our reality. His grasp of thought as an internally generated perceptual reality, moment to moment, is exceptional and he is well equipped to articulate its significance in a way that is easy to grasp but also deeply thought provoking. Adam uses this principle as a foundation from which to explore not only our personal relationship with money but also its broader implications for organisations and society at large. By additionally incorporating timeless philosophical and spiritual wisdom to support these arguments, Adam helps to bridge the gap between our minds and our relationship with money.

This is not just another book about money. It is not a financial manual; nor is it a critique of capitalism masquerading as wisdom. This is not a rant against wealth or financial success – in fact, in many ways, it is the opposite. Adam seems clear on 'What the Romans have done for us'. He is clear that money, in and of itself, is neither good nor bad; it is our relationship with money, our perceptions and misunderstandings, that dictate how it influences our lives. Adam's approach is refreshingly balanced, recognising the importance of financial systems and wealth creation while challenging many of the assumptions that we take for granted.

The book unfolds in three parts. In Part One, Adam lays the groundwork by exploring the underlying principles of human experience: how we perceive reality, how our minds function and the mechanisms that shape our understanding of the world around us. He also delves into teachings from a rich array of philosophical traditions. Drawing on Western philosophy, Eastern wisdom, Buddhism, Stoicism and more, he builds a compelling argument that challenges conventional thinking about money, success and value. This part acts as a springboard into the core of the book, where he explores various aspects of our financial lives that we often think about without a sense of clarity.

Part Two of the book brings these philosophical ideas into the real world. Here, Adam takes us on a journey through our cultural and psychological relationship with money, examining how we often perceive financial success and security versus the reality of how things truly operate. By integrating philosophy with real-life experiences and supporting his insights with anecdotal evidence from his own work with clients, Adam brings these concepts to life in a way that is both relatable and deeply impactful. Each chapter opens with a pearl of wisdom from a different tradition, guiding the reader through an exploration of familiar financial concerns – earning, spending, saving, investing – with fresh eyes and a more profound understanding.

Finally, the book zooms out to examine the bigger picture: the inherent uncertainty of life; the unpredictable nature of financial markets and economic systems; and ultimately, how we can navigate these uncertainties with greater ease and wisdom. In a world that often feels like it is spinning out of control, Adam's insights serve as an anchor, helping us to see beyond the immediate noise and confusion to something more stable, something more real.

This book is both timely and timeless. We live in an era of unprecedented financial complexity, where the traditional markers of success are being questioned and redefined. Yet at the same time, the fundamental truths about how we experience life remain unchanged. Adam has done a remarkable job of bridging these two worlds, offering insights that are both deeply philosophical and immediately practical.

For anyone seeking a clearer, more grounded relationship with money – and, by extension, with life itself – this book is an invaluable guide. I have no doubt that it will leave a lasting impact on those who engage with its wisdom, just as Adam's journey of exploration has been both a joy and an inspiration to witness.

Enjoy the journey ahead – it is one well worth taking.

Jonathan Armes
Founder and chief psychologist, Capital Shift
www.capital-shift.com
THOUGHT INTELLIGENCE®

Preface

THIS BOOK IS intended for anyone who has felt the power of money weigh on their mind and sense of peace. There is no discrimination as to whether this is caused by a lack of financial resources or an abundance thereof. It is aimed at anyone whose mind has been troubled by the burden of money and is curious as to how a more harmonious attitude might be achieved.

The interplay between mind, money and internal well-being is a fascinating and very real phenomenon. The quality and intensity of our thoughts, conditioning, belief systems and level of internal awareness shape our relationship with money dramatically – far more than we give credit for. This book is an invitation to dive more deeply into our financial decisions and take back control of how money shapes our well-being.

The early chapters of this book reflect on my own personal journey with mind and money and where we currently find ourselves. Crucially, they also explore how the mind truly works and present some supportive guiding principles from philosophy and ancient wisdom that question the current prevailing narrative. Armed with this new knowledge, we can proceed to the main section of the book, which takes us on a practical journey through various financial situations we may find ourselves in and how we might approach them. We then spend a short amount of time at the end of the book exploring how what we have learned can inform some of the bigger questions we face as human beings flying through the universe at breakneck speed on a not-so-giant rock.

I am a Chartered Financial Planner with years of experience advising individuals and families on their financial lives. I have stewarded the emotions, worries and concerns of hundreds of people and their tens of millions of collective pounds. The insights and deeply personal scenarios that I have experienced in this space compelled me to investigate and write about it. I have worked extensively with a chartered psychologist on this book for a number of years and have interviewed/surveyed clients from a vast array of socioeconomic backgrounds and financial positions. I have found this journey utterly fascinating.

This book aims to bridge the gap between the practical, financial aspects of our reality and those deepest parts of us that yearn for psychological and spiritual peace.

If money ever takes up more of your energy than you feel it needs to, this book is for you.

How this book came into being

This book is the manifestation of the personal journey that I have been on, both spiritually and financially. Like many people the world over, I have suffered from anxiety and depression – a burden that weighed me down for almost ten years. I believed that the root cause of my unhappiness was my economic situation, which at the time fell short of the life expectations I had set for myself. This section briefly explains how I arrived here and how this book came about. It is not essential to the core of the content, so if you would prefer to dive straight into things, please feel free to skip ahead.

At a very young age, I developed expectations of what my adult life would be like. I expected to graduate from university with a path to economic security carved out for me. This, I thought, was the route to fulfilment and happiness. The unknown environment on the other side, however, was quite different. I struggled to hold down a job, find my purpose and develop a career. I spent a large part of my formative years self-medicating my troubles away and pursuing a hedonistic lifestyle. I was lost, only finding a fleeting glimpse of solace in nightclubs and late-night bars as a way of numbing my low self-esteem and lack of progress both internally and out in the world.

In an attempt to escape my problems, I eventually left my home in the UK and headed for Australia, only to realise that my issues were rooted in my internal space. The prison that was my mind boarded the plane with me and didn't even have to buy a ticket. I found no freedom from this escape and returned 18 months later with more questions than the trip had answered. I knew something needed to change, but I could not pin down where my sense of worthlessness was coming from.

On my return, I met a beautiful woman who is now my wife and life partner. I was still broke and, despite meeting the woman of my dreams who would later become the mother of my incredible children, I was still lost and very low. For a long time, there was something missing, and I experienced a sense of emptiness and bruised ego. I decided to knuckle down and make something of myself, whatever that might mean.

I pinned my sense of self-worth and achievement on my economic success, thinking that would solve my problems. I embarked on a rigorous journey to gain the qualifications to become a financial planner and learn enough about money to improve my economic situation and never be unhappy again. I replaced my empty pursuit of hedonism with an almost obsessive pursuit of external validation.

Lacking a harmonious balance between mind and money at that time in my life, I also made some exuberant and reckless financial decisions along the way.

My financial situation began to change quite quickly and everything I thought I had yearned for started to come true. People were now coming to me for advice about *their* money and my career advanced in a way that I could never have expected. I was advising public figures, influencers, politicians, entrepreneurs and C-suite executives of FTSE 100 listed companies, as well as the general population. Though my 'success' was by no means to the extent you would see celebrated on TV or social media, it was a significant change from what I had been familiar with to date. At last, I had made something of myself – or so I thought.

But the feelings of discomfort, worthlessness and depression didn't go away. In fact, they got worse as the cure I was pursuing turned out to be a false remedy. I was more confused than when I started. I had assumed that the reason I felt low and unfulfilled was because I hadn't achieved the 'success' that the global narrative conditions us to believe in.

I found that my inner world was like a game of whack-a-mole. Whenever I managed to alter my external experiences to satisfy my mind's chattering, something else to worry about would pop up. It was an unwinnable game.

I didn't know this at the time, but when your mental energy is expended on unhelpful thinking, these thought patterns will permeate all areas of your life. Conversely, a clearer, less intense mind will shape your experiences in the world in a positive and dramatic way. This internal space is where all our experiences are built from.

Over the years, I tried therapy, alcohol, herbal remedies, hedonism, workaholism, the pursuit of accolades, earning, speculative investments and intellectual endeavours (to list only a few) in my attempts to find peace. But nothing worked in the same profound way as gaining a simple understanding of how my mind was bringing my experiences to life and making a concerted commitment to internal observation.

I always used to think that it's only those who have had some success who say that money doesn't buy you happiness. That's not true: they are simply the ones who know whether it does or not. When you realise it doesn't, you can be left staring into the abyss if you are still just as unhappy as you were before. It's easy to say to yourself: 'If only I could afford such-and-such, then I'd be happy.' A lack of money is an easy thing to pin your dissatisfaction on and you don't necessarily have to take your introspection any further. But getting what you thought you wanted only to find yourself in no better place forces you to ask questions.

This realisation triggered a deep intellectual and spiritual yearning for answers. 'What is the meaning of this life I am experiencing? Why is the feeling of discontent not going away?' I had everything I ever dreamed of – security, a wonderful, loving family and a challenging and rewarding career – yet I still felt empty and unfulfilled. This eventually resulted in a breakdown in front of my wife one New Year's Eve and a realisation that something needed to change.

Almost miraculously, a few short months later, I was invited to a leadership course hosted by Jonathan Armes (who has written the foreword to this book), which explored the mechanics of how the mind works in great detail. That course changed everything. I finally knew what I had to do and where I needed to look.

This is when I discovered mindfulness, the science of consciousness, spiritual teachings and philosophy. The more I learned about the true nature of my experiences in this giant playground we call Planet Earth, the more progress I started to make. Now, I am the happiest and most content I have ever been, after years of searching for answers. It's a lifelong endeavour which you never complete or completely master, but which you truly never want to stop.

The impact that this all had on me was profound. My mind became clearer; my sense of peace and security increased. I began seeing my mind for what it was and using it for its intended and powerful purpose. Of course, it is impossible to be like this all the time – that is simply unrealistic.

My business grew, my work quality improved and I wrote this book. People often said to me that they simply didn't know how I found the time or reminded me that I had a young family at home. But the most beautiful part of this is that it didn't feel overwhelming because I had more mental freedom. I was home from work on time to see my family and I didn't do anything on weekends (disclosure: I did have to write at night, but this didn't feel like a chore). I simply worked on mental decluttering, and I was able to focus much more intently and get more done in the time that I had. I was happier, less stressed and more present in the moment.

I was finally okay.

I have been influenced dramatically by a multitude of disciplines. Of course, as a Chartered Financial Planner living in the UK, I see the beneficial and attractive outputs of capitalism and a free market economy. I have also learned many of my life lessons from Eastern principles such as Buddhism and ancient Chinese wisdom. Equally, the science of mind and consciousness speaks volumes to the reality of our existence and lives; as do teachings from the ancient Greeks and Romans and all philosophers through time. To take the harmonious view of yin and yang (the beauty in balance), there is no reason why the balance of all wisdom, old and new, can't be applied to our financial lives in a Western economy (and indeed, to other aspects of our lives) to make things just that bit calmer and easier.

I now introduce some of these philosophical and spiritual principles into my business and financial planning work (for those who are interested, of course) – not only to help improve the financial situations of the individuals, families and businesses I work with, but also to make the journey a much smoother and more fulfilling one.

At first, I felt that the principles of wealth management, financial planning and philosophical inquiry were somewhat contradictory and the links between them rather tenuous; but I couldn't have been more wrong. Philosophical and spiritual principles can be applied to the monetary world with perfect harmony, so I felt compelled to write this book and share it with you.

Writing this book was a very therapeutic and enjoyable endeavour for me personally. I sincerely hope that it offers a springboard for some personal and financial growth for you too.

Yours truly,
Adam

Introduction

MONEY AND THE thoughts that go with it are all around us. Society's obsession with money and our relentless pursuit of it have led many of us to form an unhealthy relationship with it. Ideally, money should be seen as a tool to support our life's purpose; yet it often becomes the ultimate goal itself, overshadowing what truly matters.

The role of money in our lives

Our relationship with money is fraught with challenges, regardless of whether we have too much, just enough or not enough. Money generates more anxiety than most other aspects of life. After all, it is ubiquitous and we all must deal with it daily.

Society, mainstream economics and capitalism lead us to believe that the relentless pursuit and accumulation of wealth is the solution to our problems. But this mindset traps us in a cycle of desire and dissatisfaction, keeping us from true peace and fulfilment. I argue here that internal security and our financial endeavours are both worth pursuing, but they are separate matters.

In Western society, we are steeped in a culture that pushes us towards the constant pursuit of 'more'. From an early age, we are encouraged to chase financial success, status and material goods. We see these as indicators of self-worth and achievement. Our media praises gross domestic product growth as the ultimate measure of progress; while our daily conversations often revolve around career and earnings, implicitly valuing people by what they do and how much they have.

But this fixation on material success leaves many of us feeling unfulfilled. We often find ourselves on a perpetual hamster wheel, chasing happiness through promotions, possessions and pay rises. The result? A society that confuses wealth accumulation with well-being, blinding us to what really matters. We are led to believe that if we make enough money, we will find peace and satisfaction. However, the goalposts are always moving and genuine contentment remains elusive. I hope that after reading this book, you will see why that is the case.

This book aims to help you redefine your relationship with money by drawing upon the wisdom of the ancient Stoics, the teachings of the Buddha and insights from Western philosophy and spiritual leaders on the true nature of the mind. It's a journey towards understanding the deeper meaning of wealth – not just as financial capital, but as part of the broader fabric of a life well lived. By exploring these timeless perspectives, you will learn how to cultivate a healthier, more balanced approach to money, transforming it from a source of anxiety into a tool that aligns with your values and personal growth.

As a Chartered Financial Planner, I've advised individuals from all walks of life – from those struggling with debt to high-net-worth individuals caught in cycles of materialism and angst. Time and again, I've seen that it's not how much money one has, but rather one's relationship with it that shapes life satisfaction. Some of the deepest insights I've gained come not from spreadsheets but from ancient and spiritual wisdom. This has taught me that our well-being is not born from material wealth but from inner peace and self-understanding. Nevertheless, a peaceful, respectful and healthy relationship with money usually allows the mind to free itself and gain greater insight. An improved financial situation can result in more space to think clearly and logically.

As part of the preparation for this book, I surveyed over 300 people in order to explore how money interacts with their daily lives. The survey covered a broad range of individuals with a variety of occupations, incomes and levels of accessible wealth. While this book is primarily a mindful, philosophical and spiritual inquiry into money, it was important to highlight with some tangible data the power that money currently has over us.

A number of questions around money were presented to the participants and, as expected, there were some notable results that support the need for a more mindful and rational approach to our financial lives.

For example, when I asked respondents to what extent they agreed with a range of money-related statements, the survey yielded the following results (I have excluded respondents who answered neutrally):

- **"Money takes up a fair amount of my thoughts":** 73% of respondents either agreed or strongly agreed with this statement.

- **"Accumulation of money is one of my life's goals":** 52% of respondents either agreed or strongly agreed.
- **"I feel the outside world affects my inner peace":** 75% of respondents either agreed or strongly agreed.
- **"If I could remove the pressure of money, I would feel more at peace":** 76% of respondents either agreed or strongly agreed.
- **"Losing money or the prospect of having less scares me":** 77% of respondents either agreed or strongly agreed.
- **"I feel pressured to have a certain level of income or wealth":** 65% of respondents either agreed or strongly agreed.

These results indicate that for most of us, money and our experiences with it affect our inner peace to some extent.

The need for balance

This book is not about making more money or becoming rich. There are countless books on that topic already and, after reading this book, I encourage you to explore them to help increase your financial resources. Nor does this book dismiss the importance of money – it's a vital aspect of our lives and deserves respect and careful consideration. However, money should never control us or disturb our peace. Instead, this book offers tools to free you from these attachments and guide you towards a more mindful, balanced approach to your finances.

While financial hardship is a reality for many, a more liberated mindset can help to ease suffering and bring clarity to the choices we face. Worry and deliberation are time-consuming and often unhelpful, regardless of our financial situation. By embracing timeless wisdom and the reality of our experiences, we can learn to make better decisions, foster a sense of calm and perhaps even improve our financial circumstances in the process.

In this book, we will explore areas of personal finance such as debt, inheritance, retirement, investing and even our desires for material possessions. Together, we will examine the subtle ways in which we tie our self-worth and well-being to external markers of success and why the satisfaction of financial achievements is often so fleeting. In doing so, we will uncover insights that help us detach from the notion that money alone can provide happiness or a sense of purpose. Money is a source of energy and how we choose to apply that energy determines its goodness.

By the end of this journey, I hope that you will have a deeper understanding of where your beliefs about money come from and how they can be transformed. With greater freedom from these beliefs, you'll be better equipped to live a life aligned with inner peace and wisdom. Just as peaceful individuals contribute to a peaceful society, a more balanced relationship with money can lead to a more harmonious life.

In each chapter, we will return to the core theme of this book: that our well-being and sense of purpose cannot be bought but must be cultivated through an understanding of rational wisdom, the nature of our minds and modern realities. This journey will be repetitive at times, by design. Only by continuously reinforcing these principles can we make a meaningful shift in our perspective, so I invite you to embrace the process and keep an open mind.

This book is a call to re-evaluate what we seek from money, to question the relentless drive for more (without purpose) and to find greater freedom and fulfilment along the way. We will do this by exploring some tangible aspects of our financial lives that we all have to make decisions on (and often worry about). We will lean on some wisdom from Eastern, Western and spiritual teachings to parse some key areas of our financial lives and also consider their wider societal context.

The timelessness of ancient wisdom

While some Western ideologies emphasise accumulation, many ancient teachings from the East, Stoicism and other spiritual philosophies offer an alternative view. Buddhism, for instance, teaches us that inner peace comes from letting go of attachment to external rewards. It encourages a focus on *non-attachment*, suggesting that true freedom lies in finding contentment within ourselves, rather than in what we possess. Similarly, Taoism's principle of *wu wei* – acting in harmony with the natural flow of life – offers a more balanced approach to wealth and achievement. Think of it as embracing rather than fighting the inevitable flow of life.

Stoic philosophers such as Seneca and Marcus Aurelius also remind us that tranquillity comes from self-mastery and control over our desires, not from the pursuit of external wealth. These teachings underscore a powerful truth: happiness and peace aren't achieved by acquiring more, but by understanding and moderating our desires. When we approach money and wealth from this perspective, it becomes a tool to support our purpose rather than the ultimate objective of our lives.

By merging the Western drive for innovation and wealth creation with ancient philosophical and spiritual principles, we can create a more holistic approach to money. Financial success, when paired with inner peace and purpose, allows for a balanced life that honours both our material needs and our deeper sense of fulfilment.

Finally, an understanding of how our realities are shaped by thought-induced manifestations in the moment allows us to see the truth of how we experience the world and start exploring it accordingly. It is crucial that we engage with the nature of the mind and the supporting wisdom first before delving into financial matters; otherwise, this would just be another financial guidebook that does not address the core of our being. This is where our experiences can change and this is where we must look first if we want to foster a deeper, longer-lasting and more fruitful relationship with money.

A more reasoned approach

Many financial well-being books ask us simply to succumb to our financial flaws and foibles and accept that we are not rational beings. Conversely, I found that the fundamental failing of classical or mainstream economics is that it assumes that rationality is present before the mathematical models and detailed theories it expounds can work – which is, of course, a bold assumption to make. After all, we are not always rational; we are emotional beings. The field of behavioural economics has come a long way in questioning these assumptions. However, I feel that there is a more nuanced middle ground. What I am proposing is that, by calling to the nature of our experiences, we can operate from a *slightly more* rational space, which will have profound benefits for our financial lives.

This book aims to show you how to cultivate a healthy relationship with money – one that respects its power without letting it dictate your happiness. Through blending financial planning, an understanding of the mind and insights from Eastern and Western philosophy, you can find a clearer, more fulfilling path forward. This balanced approach will empower you to enjoy the fruits of your financial success while also embracing the peace, resilience and freedom that come from a grounded, rational and philosophical outlook in the present moment.

Part One

The Underlying Principles and the Power of Money

1

Money is Great, but *Why* Do We Want It?

WESTERN SOCIETY HAS a deep-rooted culture that manifests in 'more' pretty much all the time. From birth, we grow up watching those around us scrambling around for more money, higher status, keeping up with the neighbours, getting a pay rise, striving for a bigger home, buying a new car, pursuing education simply because it may unlock lucrative opportunities and many other endeavours. This all adds up to *more, more, more.* The media tells us that gross domestic product growth is a measure of our collective success; politicians tell us what 'success' means; and when we go to parties, one of the first questions we ask each other is, 'What do you do?' While there is nothing wrong with this question in and of itself, what it often means, if we're honest with ourselves, is: 'How do you make your money and how does that compare to *my* position?' It's no wonder that, entrenched as we are in a system which aligns our well-being, purpose and goals with monetary attainment, we live our lives blindly believing in this. Why would we have any reason to think otherwise? It is all we have ever known.

However, when we look closely enough, it soon becomes apparent that it isn't the car, the house, the promotion, the growth in revenue or the social status that we really want. What we're really looking for is peace of mind – and we are fooled into believing that all these external attributes (or indeed, obsessive thinking about them) will get us there.

2

Why We Give Money Such Power Over Us

HAVE YOU EVER said to yourself, your business partners, colleagues or family: 'I'll be happy when… [I buy that new car/acquire another business/get that promotion/see the market going up again/move to a bigger house]'? Have you also noticed that when you finally achieve these things, the goalposts move and you realise that the satisfaction you enjoyed was only fleeting? That's because you and your mind are on a hamster wheel, looking at your personal wellness and satisfaction from an 'outside-in' perspective (more on that later).

When you ask people *why* they want these things, their answers are usually very similar. They almost always say, 'Because it will make me feel secure,' or 'It'll take the pressure off,' or 'It will make me feel more comfortable.'

When you look at this more closely, it's apparent that what we're all really striving for is peace, stillness and security *in our minds.*

To put it simply, we're making ourselves crazy in attempting to make ourselves *not* crazy!

This does not mean that achievements, growth, financial gain and innovation are not worth pursuing. It's just not true that achieving these things will bring you internal peace. Jim Carrey once famously said, "I wish everyone could get rich and famous and everything they ever dreamed of so they can see that's not the answer."

The route to freedom, as I will argue many times in these pages, is an internal pursuit. This is where we must look to achieve it.

This book will show you that this stillness is within you already and can never come from any monetary endeavour out there in the world. This idea may seem rather obscure right now, but it will become much clearer as you read on. Once you grasp it, you can start to develop a much healthier, more controlled and respectful relationship with money for yourself, your organisation and as a collective member of society.

Once you learn that you can be more peaceful now, rather than 'when…', it will help to create a clearer, freer space for you to make financial decisions in a more pragmatic and respectful way, rather than being driven by thoughts, emotions and attachments.

This may mean realising that you do in fact have enough to retire on or that you can work out what more needs to be done to get you there. It could mean that you understand that most of the stuff you buy doesn't in fact make you any happier at all, and that you can stabilise your budget more and invest for the future. It could mean that the innovation that your business is working on is worthwhile after all, despite the risks. It could also mean the opposite. The point of this is that a looser relationship between money and mind will allow you to approach your financial decisions not through emotion or attachment, but from the part of the mind that optimal decisions come from.

3

What Does a Healthy Position Look Like?

UNDERSTANDING HOW THE mind works affords very subtle yet extremely profound benefits in our daily lives. In this book, I explore how this can apply to the world of money. Money is a great way to showcase this, simply because it is such a central and influential force in the outside world. The learnings, however, can improve all aspects of our lives by helping us to find a bit more quietude and serenity.

Once we've explored this, we will still face the same outside world, but we'll have a completely new and calmer way of dealing with it. Something different awaits that we can look forward to.

Peace

Getting to grips with the reality of your experiences will create some space in your mind. With this space comes the ability to think more clearly and gain insights into what really matters to you. Knowing the truth about the relationship between your thoughts and your experiences will allow you to approach the ways of the world with greater focus and clarity.

When it comes to your money, you will have the space to make clearer, more effective choices; understand where you are and where you are going; and maintain a healthy distance between your financial situation and your sense of well-being. You will be able to find comfort in your financial life, however it may look.

From this position of comfort, you can start asking questions such as, 'Okay, so what do I do from here?', rather than getting tied up in a continuous mental spiral of, 'I don't have enough/I could lose it all/I can't pay the bills/My home is going to get repossessed/The business could go under/I have failed my children/I need more money to be happy/I don't know what to do with all this money.'

Financial stress, worry and emotion take myriad different forms for the rich and the poor, but the principle remains the same. Once you realise how this unhelpful thinking manifests, you will be free from the burdensome hold it has over you and will enjoy a more peaceful life and relationship with money.

Creativity

Once you have been released from these shackles, a new freedom awaits.

Loosening that addiction to the pay cheque, the 10% salary raise for a 40% increase in working hours or the bragging rights that come with an extra bedroom will afford you more room in your mind for fresh thinking. Nothing need be forced or premeditated: this fresh thinking will allow you to approach your life more creatively.

It may be that you have new ideas for the career path you want to pursue, or that investing those extra 40% of hours into your passions will enable you to more easily improve or optimise your financial position. It may be that letting go of your attachment to the figure on your pay cheque for just one year will allow you to run with that risky but beautiful and innovative idea you've always wanted to pursue. It may be that you think of a way to be more efficient in your current role or in your family budget to free up some money for your future planning.

When your mind is racing around the same old ideas and is filled with compulsive worry or obsession over money, its energy is being consumed. Letting go, even if ever so slightly, creates some space for new ideas to emerge – and it may just be that these new ideas result in more money!

Joy and awe

When you pull back the curtains on how your mind works, more space for joy and awe becomes available to you. The (more often than not) Wild West of your mind when it is overly affected by the outside world can leave very little room to think and feel anything else. This doesn't just relate to money; it relates to almost anything that you deliberate and worry about. It just happens to be that money is way up there on the list of things that we allow to influence our experience of life.

Understanding the realities of how your mind works will enable you not only to put some distance between your well-being and your money, but also to create more space to see the beauty that is all around you in your everyday life.

Growth

I discussed earlier how an obsession with 'growth' has been ingrained in all of us by powerful societal influences. Please do not misunderstand the purpose of this book. There is nothing wrong with growth: it has given us great privileges in life, helping us to live longer, giving us employment, moving people out of poverty and providing memorable experiences.

The problem with growth arises when you see it as a tool to give you 'well-being' or 'purpose'. This is not the case. I argue in this book that growth – and money, for that matter – is a very important part of our societal system and we should treat it with respect. The point is this: with a healthier relationship between our minds and our attitude to money, we will free up space to innovate more, grow more and become more creative.

The anchor that money can place on our well-being can hinder our ability to perform better, rather than catalyse it. There is no trade-off here.

Think of this as an example: I have an opportunity to grow my business, get a promotion or make a financial investment for my future. I can't bring myself to do so because there is a small risk of financial loss in the first few years. I decide not to go ahead because I'm afraid that the number on the screen or the balance sheet may become smaller. As this would be disturbing, I decide not to act because of the short-term impact on my financial position and thus my well-being.

Can you see how this emotional attachment to money is actually *anti-growth*? By adopting a looser relationship between the figures on the screen and the sense of well-being that you place on them, you end up with a greater ability to grow. This example also illustrates how money can control you in the opposite way, letting you take uncalculated and damaging risks simply because you're driven by the emotional influence that your mind places on the financial decision in front of you. By detaching slightly, you will be able to look at these decisions much more clearly from a place of calm and rationality, rather than being driven by unhelpful thoughts. You will then know that whatever the outcome, the decision was the right one at the time, with no regrets.

Wisdom

Understanding how you form your experiences will not only free your mind but also help you to gain wisdom in your daily life. The mind is a powerful intellectual tool that can either be a great help or a great hindrance to you. Together, we will explore some pearls of wisdom from significant historical and more recent thinkers that have stood the test of time, permeated throughout cultures and are still overwhelmingly relevant today – particularly around our relationship with money.

4

The Current State of Play

APOLOGIES, BUT BEFORE we go any further, we must first pause and look at where we find ourselves right now.

The world, including the people in it, is a beautiful place. There is no denying this. It's a cosmic miracle that the world exists at all — even disregarding the fact that you, as an individual, have an infinitesimal probability of ever being around to witness it. The odds of you existing as you, at this time, reading this book, are so unbelievably small that they're as close to impossible as makes little difference. However, most would agree that we are living at a time of great uncertainty, discontent and torment all over the world. There have been global conflicts, pandemics, inflation crises, trade wars, bank failures, market crashes, political polarisation and ideological wars in the last five years alone. It's easy to see why we might let this uncertainty impact our experiences of the world. In my work of overseeing people's money, I have seen this all too often.

We will explore how our current relationship with money underpins how we relate to some of these issues; but the insights that we uncover here can, of course, be applied to many other aspects of our lives.

By design, I will not labour on the world's ills in any more detail. While there are many problematic situations out there in society, the whole premise of this book is to create some space between an outside world fuelled by an obsession with money and your own inner peace (for the benefit of both your financial life and wider society). With that said, it's important to define where we find ourselves right now, so that we can appreciate what's on offer on the other side.

On a personal level, we are constantly in a state of flux when it comes to money matters. When we let our emotions drive our financial decisions, we can often make illogical or suboptimal choices. This can apply to many things that we make decisions about, such as education, risk, career options, healthcare and well-being, relationships, saving for the future, investing money, taking on debt or planning for retirement (among others).

The truth is that when we let our thoughts manifest into an emotionally charged decision-making process, we can often look at various money matters incorrectly. For example, when we are driven by fear of volatility in the financial markets, we may decide not to invest money that we won't need for 20 years simply through fear of a fluctuating value, despite the overwhelming long-term financial benefits of such investing thus far in history. A clearer, freer mind could approach this logically and ask questions such as: 'Does the balance of probability of long-term economic growth and human innovation outweigh the probability that those days are over and nothing good will ever happen again?'

The same goes for debt. The word 'debt' can come with negative connotations; but if it liberates your financial life, it can be a good thing. Mortgages for home purchases are a prime example. Anxiety around debt may prevent you from taking on that innovative venture, securing a family home or seizing an opportunity. We can also say the same for poor debt decisions, such as borrowing for a venture out of nothing but excitement and an inadequate appraisal of the reality of what is in front of you. Until we understand where these decisions and outcomes derive from, we will always be driven by a messy mind. This messy mind does not help our financial lives – it hinders them.

Particularly in Western society, we often buy things that we don't need to impress people we don't know or to fit in with the majority. We intrinsically understand this, but it doesn't stop us from pursuing the status symbol, indulging in retail therapy or making an impulse buy. There is a reason for this. We are trying to feel at peace and the short-term relief provided by these things may just help us do that, until the next need for gratification or status soon comes up. As a result, some people can land in trouble through credit card dependency, stress, mental health problems and a constant need to 'keep up' or work in a job they hate because they 'need' the salary. It can also affect sound decision-making around, for example, saving and investing for the future, starting a new creative venture or reducing your debt exposure, which can lead to potential opportunity cost.

This book aims to create a little bit of mental freedom for you – a clarity that will help you to understand how your mind really works, lean into some tried-and-tested wisdom from the ages and investigate how some of your decisions arise so that you can approach your financial life in a more considered way.

We currently attach a lot of our self-worth to money and measure our 'success' by our financial achievements and the attention we get from others. When we take this approach, influenced by the outside world, it can lead to problematic relationships with ourselves. This can result in decisions or attachments that aren't good for us. I'm not going to talk too much about this, as it's fairly obvious that, out there in the world, we have issues with the cult of fame and celebrity, the 'me' culture, toxic masculinity, rising suicide rates, climate change and the environment, addictions (gambling, porn, drugs, obesity) and domestic violence.

The list is long.

While this book focuses on our mind and our money, money is also influential in many of these wider societal themes. If more actors in society had freer, clearer, more peaceful minds, this could have a profound impact on the state of affairs in which we currently find ourselves. All of this is achievable and need not stop us from pursuing our financial goals or respecting money in a way that is appropriate and allows us to function properly in the world today.

It's true that this book has been written to help individuals and families to develop a more appropriate relationship with money. I would be remiss, however, if I didn't highlight the obvious relationship between money and societies the world over. After all, individuals make up the societies we all live in.

The global issues that we face are profound. You know this already. Our relationship (obsession) with money is central, or at least significantly influential, to many of the issues that we currently face. We face widening inequality, environmental damage, corruption, over-exploitation of resources, climate change, lack of regulation in important sectors, technological risks, geopolitical instability, multiple political crises and many more challenges that would merit a whole book in themselves. The world, as I've already said, is a beautiful miracle in itself, but we do have some problems.

The point is: if our relationship with money influences many of these issues, then adjusting this relationship could at least start to address some of these problems from the bottom up – that is, starting with you as an individual.

5

The True Nature of How We Experience Life and Money

I AM BY NO means a qualified psychologist or neuroscientist, but I was fortunate enough to spend a lot of time with a leading chartered psychologist while preparing to write this book. In 2022, I attended one of Capital Shift's leadership retreats in the beautiful Welsh countryside, where the reality of how our minds work was explored in great detail. Subsequently, I explored the topic of mind and money with Jonathan Armes (the chief psychologist and founder of Capital Shift) for around two years as I planned this book.

Under Jonathan's stewardship, it became clear to me that all our experiences are formed from the inside out: our minds simply take in sensory information from the outside world and interpret that information through thoughts and feelings, which shape how we experience the world. You can liken this to the mind being a projector, taking in information and then projecting reality out onto the world. This is how we live and how reality is shaped for each and every one of us. This is contrary to our common belief that the world happens to us and determines how we experience it. If we want to change the projection, we must look at the projector.

Many of us currently believe that the external world is what informs *how* we experience our lives. We believe that our well-being is constantly influenced by outside events. What is ultimately true, however, is that, through the reality of our conscious experiences, we merely take in sensory information from the outside world and try to make sense of what is out there. We receive this information and have some thoughts around it, which generate feelings. Those feelings subsequently lead to the experiences that we have out in the world at any given moment. This is subtly but profoundly different from what we often (almost automatically) think. *We are the architects of how we experience the world through our minds.* Or, to put it differently: *We bring our experiences into being through thought.* Thoughts and feelings are transient and emerge in the moment. Understanding this can liberate us from the power that these may hold over our financial decision-making and life experiences, with a view to gaining more control over them.

The reason we all see and experience the world differently is because we are simply receiving inputs and trying to make sense of them, based on our past experiences. As we all have different past experiences, we all see and experience things differently. You only need to look at historic economic predictions to know that simulating the past isn't very good at forecasting the future. Perhaps it's the same with our minds!

When I ask my wife to imagine the most beautiful and soul-replenishing scene, she will tell me that she is by the ocean, listening to the waves and feeling the sand in her hands. But when I try to picture that scene, I see mountain tops, jagged rock edges and trees growing out from the mountainside, with the sound of the wind permeating my eardrums. What is the truth here? There really isn't a fundamental truth: we just interpret and process information differently and ultimately have our own versions of what reality is to us and how it makes us feel. Neither is right or wrong. Many leading neuroscientists now describe reality as some form of controlled hallucination in an attempt to make sense of what is around us, thus supporting the fact that our 'reality' is an internal construct. If it is indeed internal, then we get some power back through how we choose to perceive, interpret and interact with the outside world (including dealing with money).

Let's incorporate some tangible financial examples. Think of a crash in the financial markets that temporarily reduces the value of your investments. A very common response to this is a negative one which can interfere with your well-being. The true reality is that it's just a temporary position and just a number (it's just information).

Some investors love financial crashes because they are able to buy more investments at a lower cost – almost like seeing the car they've always wanted with 30% off the price for a short time. Some find crashes very problematic, interfering with their mental state and feeling of security. They contemplate selling their investments (so that they can feel okay and secure).

Which position is correct? The truth is that the event itself (the crash) is neither good nor bad – it just *is*. How we experience and interact with the event depends on how our minds interpret it through thought, which influences our feelings and thus our experience. That experience is simply a projection of how our minds have decided to interpret the event. It is our own construct.

Recognising this simple but profound truth eventually gives you more control over how you deal with the sensory information that you receive. It may mean that, actually, you let the market crash do what it needs to, with your well-being firmly intact, avoiding the costly mistake of selling at a loss simply to pacify your negative thoughts. It may mean that you have the capacity to turn a crisis into an opportunity.

Before I started out on my own journey along this path, I couldn't even stand in a queue for anything without getting incredibly frustrated and stressed. Today, I love queuing for absolutely anything because it gives me another opportunity to observe my thoughts and have a moment of peace and introspection. Queues have now become something I rather enjoy. This is a silly and light-hearted example, but it shows how a fresh perspective on something can lead to a completely different experience. Apply this to our financial lives, which we will get to shortly, and significant changes can emerge.

Our conscious state is inherently still and calm by its very design. It's the thoughts from our minds that then do the work of interpreting our experiences. Noticing this in real time is where true personal growth and wisdom start to come to life. From this place, you can work towards making much better financial decisions.

To build on the difference between our still, calm and aware state of consciousness and our thought-driven mind, we will explore a couple of scenarios.

Think of a scenario where you are fully embraced in the moment and have total clarity. This could be when you turn a corner to see the most beautiful sunset with all its oranges, pinks and dark shades of blue. All the mental clutter disappears and you are simply in awe of the beauty in front of you. For that brief moment, there are no thoughts, worries or mental business. Everything is calm and tranquil. Or this could occur during a state of grave difficulty, such as a car accident, a health emergency or a problem involving your children.

When such an event is happening and you're 'in it', time seems to stop, as do your thoughts: you are fully engaged in the moment and what needs to be done. You are not panicking. The mind does not begin to assess potential future concerns until the intensity of the moment has passed.

This can also happen when you're deeply engaged in and focused on something – for example, music, work or listening to a friend. You may be so engrossed in the moment that you have no idea where the time has gone and realise that, during this brief but fleeting window, there were no thoughts, worries or deliberations in your mind. You may be busy or working hard, but you're calm and your mind is still.

There are many other instances of this, but the reason for exploring it is simple: your inner self has a still and tranquil place that *can* be accessed. It is undoubtedly there; but at first, it may seem very hard to reach when the outside world bombards us with so many distracting and intrusive stimuli.

There are some financial events that happen in our lives which we would prefer to avoid. I do not seek to take anything away from that. Losing a job or a loved one, having your home repossessed or dealing with a gambling catastrophe – these are not outcomes that you would choose; nor is anyone arguing that you get to simply decide how happy you are after such outcomes. However, it is still true that each event and how it is perceived is entirely interpreted by you: moments move to new moments, which generate new thoughts, experiences and interpretations.

In a bad situation, you may just be able to find some clarity to take some helpful next steps. This is far better than suffering from a crippling inner state over what has already happened and can't be changed. If the thoughts are negative, the experience will continue to be negative. If they are instead shaped positively to focus on what can be done, the experience will become a more positive one and will compound over time.

In moments of financial stress, recognition that feelings of panic, fear or disturbance are temporary can provide the space needed to approach problems with clarity and rationality rather than acting on the panic itself.

The significance of this simple fact is that the external world (financial or otherwise) is not the root cause of our experiences. It's our *thoughts* around money or the external world that generate our emotional responses, which ultimately dictate how we interpret an experience. Rationally, we know this to be true. An easy way to evidence this is to look again at how different individuals can have completely different experiences of the same financial situation: a poor person can live with joy or resentment; a rich person can be happy or miserable. Some of the happiest people I have worked with have much less in nominal financial terms than some of the unhappiest people I have worked with. This isn't always the case, but it's true in such a high number of instances that one must conclude that well-being and money are not as closely intertwined as many of us think. It's more a state-of-mind phenomenon than an external one. After all, *how* we experience the events in our life is entirely interpreted by our own minds, so how could it be any other way? Life out there happens to all of us in different ways, but how we interpret our experiences is entirely up to us.

Let's take a look at the responses of two different people to the Covid-19 pandemic as an example of how our thoughts give rise to our experiences. What we will look at here affected many people. The stock market reduced in value significantly in March 2020.

- Person A decided to sell out of their £100,000 initial investment at a 30% loss because their mind was telling them that this would keep them safe amid all the uncertainty. Person A's thoughts led to a feeling of insecurity and an action to opt out of that uncertainty. They withdrew £70,000 to their bank account.
- Person B's thoughts were that markets have crashed before and have always, thus far, gone on to recover. They also thought that this could be a good time to add to their portfolio and invested another £10,000. They put the money in and went about their lives, removed from the noise.

What different realities had these initial, yet very different thoughts brought into being six months later? Person A had £81,750 (their bank balance plus six months' interest at 5% and the same £10,000 spare cash that person B had available). Person B had £113,000 (the market went on to fully recover and they added £10,000, which grew by 30% during the recovery).

That's a £31,250 difference. I have been kind on person A here and have not undertaken a 20-year comparison. Two very different realities emerged from two very different thought responses to exactly the same stimulus or information. This is the power of thought; and this is why we must look here first for personal and financial growth. It all starts with our thoughts – and our experiences come into being from those very thoughts. This is both staggeringly simple and staggeringly beautiful.

When my own clients were panicking during this time, helping them to change their thinking around the issue before actions and experiences came into being saved some of them an awful lot of money. It required no technical competence from me whatsoever; their thinking changed and so did their realities. They did this all on their own by applying a rational approach and detaching their sense of security from the values on their dashboards.

And it doesn't stop there. The power of thought manifests different outcomes in all areas of our financial lives. How you think about debt, hardship, budgeting, inheritance, risk and everything else has profound impacts. Two people with two different thoughts will go on to have two very different experiences. The good news is that with a bit of observation, you can work on your thoughts and thus your reality.

Understanding this truism affords more freedom to cultivate a healthier inner environment when approaching financial decisions. Ultimately, the ideal situation is to have a high level of personal well-being *and* strong financial security. The latter is much harder to achieve without the former. Much of the literature out there on money is about using it to achieve freedom. The premise here is that the freedom comes first, enabling an individual to be better equipped to navigate the world of money in an easier, more advantageous way.

The mind is an inherently powerful tool but, left unchecked, this power can be exhausted on the same old repetitive thinking. Worry, anxiety and deliberation consume a lot of energy; and if the mind's energy is being expended in this way, there is little room for the fresh, insightful (not to mention profitable) thinking which is a much better use of this invaluable tool that we have at our disposal.

Many of the arguments throughout this book stem from the reality of how our minds work and how we experience the world through our perceptions and projections. There is extensive literature out there on the science of consciousness and what the relationship between our minds and the outside world really looks like. I strongly encourage you to explore these fascinating works after you have read this book. They will do a far better job of explaining things than I am qualified or able to do.

In the following chapters, we will explore some pearls of wisdom from the ages that support this concept of how our experiences are formed. It may seem a bit 'out there' at first and a little counterintuitive to your current view of how things work; but by exploring some teachings that have prevailed across cultures and throughout the centuries, we can examine how the nature of our minds works within our financial lives.

We've already seen that the power of thought coming into being informs our experiences. You may be thinking that you can't help how you think, but that's not necessarily true. Your opinions and thoughts about people, places, foods, social settings, partners and money have probably not been fixed your entire life, so there is an inherent ability to change your thinking – or, more importantly, an ability to allow new thoughts or fresh perspectives to emerge.

The reason why you may have read money books historically with a view to bettering your financial position, only to find that you don't follow or stick to their guidance, is that you probably haven't been getting to the root of the issue. The root is your inner space where you think, which subsequently leads to your outcomes. Hints, tips and strategies are great; but without a fundamental understanding of how your thoughts influence your existence, this pursuit is often futile. Furthermore, simply accepting your limitations as a flawed human being isn't necessary; you can change how you experience the world by cultivating a calmer inner space. It is possible.

When new tricks, hacks or tools are added to a messy mind full of unhelpful or unproductive thoughts, it's no wonder that so few of us manage to make meaningful financial change or find this more difficult than a self-help book would suggest.

We have never had so much information, social media advice, artificial intelligence tools, blogs, books and videos at our fingertips. However, people are still left baffled as to why they cannot solve the age-old problem of how to overcome financial restriction. It's because they have not been working on the very starting point of all their experiences: their thoughts and, by extension, their mind's work.

We can do this by delving into philosophical wisdom and embracing the beauty of self-inquiry through practising mindfulness, which we will come on to shortly.

It turns out that many ancient traditions have been scrutinising this very phenomenon over thousands of years.

6

The Wisdom of the Stoics

THE STOICS – including philosophers such as Seneca, Marcus Aurelius and Epictetus – offer profound insights into managing the challenges of life, including our relationship with money. Their teachings emphasise the importance of focusing on what we can control – our thoughts, choices and reactions – while letting go of what lies beyond our influence. This perspective is deeply relevant to developing a freer relationship with money, a concept that is often influenced by the external world and all its uncertainties.

Financial setbacks, market volatility and economic uncertainty are all part of life. The Stoic approach teaches us that while these external events are beyond our control, how we respond to them is entirely within our power. In his famous *Meditations*, Marcus Aurelius wrote: "You have power over your mind – not outside events. Realise this, and you will find strength." This mindset can transform the way we handle money. Instead of reacting with fear or anxiety to financial losses or challenges, or responding through greed, comparison or ego, we can adopt a resilient approach and focus on the rational and practical implications.

Stoicism also warns against the trap of excessive desire. Seneca observed that wealth does not bring happiness but often breeds greater dissatisfaction, as those who crave wealth can never have enough. He argued that true wealth comes from appreciating what we already have and focusing on living virtuously rather than acquiring more. This aligns closely with the idea that financial freedom is not about amassing wealth but about achieving peace of mind. Again, there is nothing inherently right or wrong about acquiring wealth and building your financial resources; but doing so through desire and aligning these with your sense of well-being is where the mental trapdoor starts to open.

A Stoic approach to money encourages us to use wealth wisely, treating it as a tool rather than a master. Epictetus reminds us that the pursuit of external goods such as money and status often leads us further from the good life by distracting us from the virtues, such as wisdom, justice and self-control. These, he argues, are what truly matter. By practising such virtues, we can achieve a sense of inner freedom that external circumstances, including our financial situation, cannot undermine. We will explore the ideas of some of these great thinkers in later chapters by aligning some of their wise words with real-world examples from our financial lives.

Ultimately, Stoicism teaches us that financial freedom begins with the mind. By focusing on what we can control and ensuring our financial decisions are informed by our values, we can build a healthier relationship with money. This perfectly aligns with our exploration of how the mind works and the realities of how our experiences are formed. Stoic philosophy has been relevant to human life for thousands of years; as have the wise words of the Buddha...

7

The Tranquillity of Buddhism

Buddhism offers timeless insights into the nature of desire, attachment and the pursuit of happiness. All of these, of course, are deeply relatable to our relationship with money. A core Buddhist principle is the idea that *dukkha* (suffering) arises from *tanha* (craving or attachment). Buddhism argues that the cause of all suffering is desire.

This craving can often manifest as a desire for material wealth, status or external validation, which we often believe is the key to our internal sense of security. What we will learn from these principles, and the reality of how our minds work, is that we have had the tools for financial peace (and peace in general) all along.

In a financial sense, this craving can take the form of constantly striving for more – more income, more possessions, more security – without questioning whether these pursuits align with our core values or where the deeper part of us, from which such desires derive, lies. Buddhism reminds us that such attachment is a source of suffering, as it creates an insatiable cycle of desire that can never be truly satisfied because there is no end point. As soon as one goal is achieved, another emerges, leaving us perpetually dissatisfied. The solution, according to Buddhist teachings, lies in cultivating *non-attachment*. This doesn't mean rejecting money or material goods but rather approaching them with a sense of balance and perspective, knowing that your well-being is intact with or without them.

Mindfulness – another key Buddhist practice and a growing practice in wider society – offers a powerful tool for transforming our relationship with money. By observing our thoughts and emotions without judgement, we can identify patterns of fear, greed, envy or insecurity that influence our financial decisions. Paying close attention to how your mind is generating these feelings is a huge step.

This is not to say that these thoughts and emotions will stop (they won't); but knowing what they are and how they have manifested enables a fundamental change. It allows you to notice how these thoughts are manifesting, which will help you to create some space for fresher thinking. For example, a mindful approach might reveal that a desire to buy an expensive car is driven not by genuine need, interest or passion, but by a longing for social status.

With this awareness, we can make more deliberate choices. Again, this is not to say that buying an expensive car is inherently good or bad; it's the *why* that matters. If it's because of envy and an insecure ego, perhaps it's not such a good idea. But if you love the car and admire the engineering, it's a much more values-driven decision.

Generosity, or *dana*, is also central to Buddhist teachings and offers a way to counteract attachment. By giving – whether through charitable donations, acts of kindness or helping family members at important life stages – we can break the cycle of self-centred craving and use our money with more purpose and meaning. Money is a powerful energy that can complement our lives if we let it.

Buddhism teaches that true happiness and freedom come from within. By embracing mindfulness, non-attachment and generosity, we can transform our relationship with money, using it as a tool to support a life of purpose and meaning rather than as a measure of our worth or well-being. These principles are not just universal to Buddhism either, as we're about to find out.

8

A Fundamental Truth as Old as Time

THE PURSUIT OF wealth and security is as old as civilisation itself. Across other ancient cultures, thinkers and philosophers grappled with questions about the role of money in a good life. Their wisdom remains strikingly relevant today, offering timeless principles for building a healthier relationship with wealth.

Aristotle's concept of the 'golden mean' is a cornerstone of ancient Greek philosophy. He argued that virtue lies in balance, avoiding extremes of excess and deficiency. Applied to money, this means finding a middle ground between reckless extravagance and obsessive hoarding. Aristotle viewed wealth as a means to an end, not an end in itself, emphasising that the ultimate goal is *eudaimonia*: a flourishing life filled with purpose and virtue. This perspective challenges the modern fixation on accumulation, reminding us to focus on what money enables us to do rather than stopping short at money being the end point in itself.

Ancient Chinese wisdom argues for balance (think yin and yang). Ancient Rome had deep philosophical thinkers who very much agreed with the Stoics on the need to exercise self-control over our emotions. Christianity and the Bible emphasise that our hearts are where we place our treasure. Hindus have deep philosophy on the mind, body and soul. Islam teaches a need to reason and use logical processes to approach decisions. These common cultural underpinnings reveal a fundamental consistency in all of this.

While many cultures have ideological differences, the spiritual exploration of the mind and our approach to life is fairly consistent in the broadest sense and can be applied to our daily lives, whatever our philosophical, religious or personal leanings may be. You don't need to belong to any particular faction or belief system to benefit from this cross-cultural wisdom. Embracing this wisdom enables you to find out for yourself that there is indeed an easier space available for you. This is what we will look at next.

9

The Real Meaning of Mindfulness and Spiritual Inquiry

DON'T LET THE word 'spiritual' spook you. It is often misunderstood or misconstrued as religious fervour. Spiritual endeavours are not merely reserved for traditional religions, doctrines or ancient texts. The practice of spiritual inquiry, in this context, simply means investing time and energy in self-reflection, contemplating the universe and your place in it, and freeing your mind by observing it through your consciousness.

This concept aligns deeply with the message of this book. Your relationship with money is not just about external gains or losses but also about how you perceive, react to, and find meaning in the financial aspects of your life. Mindfulness or spirituality as an endeavour invites you to approach your financial decisions – and indeed, your entire life – with a sense of curiosity and detachment. By doing so, you create the mental clarity needed to make better choices while maintaining a sense of inner peace.

In the same way that spiritual inquiry encourages us to explore our inner worlds, it also helps us to recognise the impermanence of the external world. Our thoughts and emotions around money, like everything else, are fleeting. By stepping back and observing these feelings, we gain freedom from the undue power that they hold over us (by not taking them so seriously). This is not dissimilar to ancient teachings across various spiritual traditions, which encourage letting go of attachments to achieve a higher state of being. Whether it's the Buddhist principle of non-attachment, the Stoic practice of observing emotions without judgement or the Christian call to lay treasures in heaven, the underlying message is the same: true freedom comes from within; and from that place of freedom, new experiences can come into being. Your financial experiences are no different.

Spiritual endeavour invites you to adopt a broader perspective. When you step back and observe the impermanence of all things, money included, you gain the ability to focus on what truly matters. This practice doesn't require you to adhere to a particular doctrine or belief system. It only asks that you remain curious, reflective and open to exploring the relationship between your inner state and the world around you.

People can embark on this journey in a multitude of ways – for example, yoga, fasting, practising gratitude, manifesting, breathing exercises, general mindfulness, meditation, listening to guided meditation podcasts or simply observing the mind and how thoughts and experiences emerge. However you do it, finding a way to check into the stillness that is inherent in your consciousness (before thoughts come in) allows you to observe your mind from a seat of impartiality. Even if this is only momentary, it confirms that the mind can be completely tranquil. It is transient and impermanent thoughts and feelings that disturb it, and these are things of our own making. Exercising some strength over how seriously you take your thoughts and manifestations will allow you to position yourself more purposefully when addressing the world of money.

It is the best investment that you can make.

Have you ever noticed yourself thinking a lot? Have you ever said to yourself, 'I'm really in my head today,' or 'I can't get this out of my head'? Which part of you is noticing that? You can't smell your own nose, so there's another part of you that is rationally observing the deliberation of your mind.

This, again, is where we must look.

For me, meditation – along with my work with Jonathan Armes – played a key role in helping to take the edge off the impact of the outside world on my internal well-being. It allowed me to see for myself that what I had learned about the mind was true. It separated 'me' from my mind (at least some of the time!). I was able to watch my thoughts and my mind without judgement and at that point, I truly understood that there is a perfectly calm place in there somewhere, and that accessing this place could be very beneficial in my daily life, including my financial life. I also found that by not seeing my thoughts as some absolute truth but accepting that they simply emerge in the moment and are transient, I gained some control over their intensity and the ability to look at things differently. My mind became clearer and stopped trying so hard to manipulate the world around me or make everything okay through deliberation.

My idea to write this book was born out of that mental space; but it would not have happened historically, when I falsely believed that the world out there was dictating how I experienced it.

How you go about all this, however, is up to you. There is no right or wrong answer; all I ask is that you simply observe and spend some time looking at how your thoughts, and thus your experiences, come into being. Just watch. That's all you need to do. You will regain the higher ground as the observer and may not take your mind's deliberations as seriously. Thoughts will come and go with greater ease and less attachment, leaving room for new thoughts that you may just like a whole lot more. You're the boss – you get to decide what you do and don't listen to.

Spirituality is about looking inwards for our peace, rather than outwards. We know already that the mind, and thus our experiences out there in the world, work from the inside out. That is where we must look for our security. The beauty of this is that you don't need to take my word for it: you can go and find out for yourself.

You may at this point be thinking, 'Okay, I understand the principle, but I can't help my thoughts – so what's the point in saying all this?' It's true that thoughts come and go, and we never know what they're going to be. We are all subject to our mind's natural methodology of drawing on past experiences to attempt to solve present and future problems. The difference now is that you understand that thoughts come and go from moment to moment. You understand that the mind is simply trying to make sense of whatever stimuli it is receiving, and that there is a still place in there that you can visit while observing this happening in real time. In so doing, you can take each thought that passes through less seriously and let go of the thought sooner if it is not productive, useful or true (how many times have you worried about something that never happened? Almost always?!). A less attached approach allows new, different thoughts to emerge, which may be more helpful. This, of course, is how different or more advantageous financial outcomes can arise.

It's not about forcing changes in thinking or altering thought patterns using brute force (that isn't possible); what is possible is increasing our awareness of thoughts coming and going. We then have more power over whether we let those thoughts manifest, whether we bring them to life in the outside world or not. Watching them come and go with less attachment can bring about genuine change in how we view our minds and what we use them for.

With more space to allow for fresh thinking, new and different experiences can emerge. Over time, your mind gains a more diverse dataset of experiences to work from, which compounds over time, rather than going over the same old ground.

With mental and spiritual compounding intact, dealing with financial compounding becomes a whole lot easier.

10

Western Ideology

It is true that the modern, Western world seemingly places more value on wealth accumulation and materialism than other societies (and indeed, more than previous civilisations and historical epochs). Liberal individualism has been the order of the day in the West since the Enlightenment. While the underlying economic structure of the West may seem contradictory to other traditions and teachings, the role of individual responsibility for one's mind, rationality and financial relationships is a subtle but important continuation of the same principles. We are ultimately the crafters of all our experiences; and with this responsibility, we can begin to work on a healthier approach.

It is also undeniable that life in the Western world relies on the growth and accumulation model to survive. We need to get out there and earn money to eat, heat, thrive and retire. This naturally involves the pursuit of financial (not mental) security and participation in a capitalist structure – a structure that has brought us no end of technological, medical and life expectancy benefits over the decades. I am not dismissing the value of Western capitalism; quite the contrary. We get to live longer, cure diseases and access a wealth of information at our fingertips. We can thank capitalism for much of that. But by understanding our minds and incorporating some wisdom that has lasted through the ages, we can interact with the system with greater tranquillity and get more out of it, while also enjoying the ride.

What does all this mean? Let's tie it all together before we look at some real-life examples.

11

Combining the Principles

My argument – and the entire premise of this work – rests on how to utilise the aforementioned principles to ensure that we can achieve our financial goals and maintain or improve our well-being in tandem. We all intrinsically understand that balance, moderation and compromise are fundamental ingredients for healthy outcomes, and applying these principles in a balanced way is no different. With a freer, more rational mind, there is room for a healthy detachment of well-being from money. The anxious and emotionally led experiences that you have with money do not profit your well-being – or indeed, your financial situation. With an arm's-length approach to the numbers on the screen, you have a clearer headspace to make better financial decisions and get closer to your financial goals, while making the journey much easier in the process.

Understanding how the mind works and influences your experience is a good intellectual starting point. Philosophical wisdom allows you to further explore that understanding; while practising mindfulness (or spiritual inquiry) allows you to see it for yourself and *feel* the benefits.

This is why we need to explore all this before looking at anything else. This is why ancient wisdom is still so relevant today. This is why introspection and mindfulness have profound benefits for our lives. It's because the human mind and our experience of reality haven't changed. Everything that we experience is manifested internally and then projected back out onto the world (i.e. from the inside out). That's why external manipulations (new jobs, cars, houses, investments, businesses) seldom give us the peace we originally thought they would. We've been looking at this the wrong way round our entire lives.

Armed with these principles, we can now start to examine the areas of our finances that we must regularly contend with to see how understanding the true nature of these situations makes them far easier to navigate.

With an understanding of how the mind works, we have the insight and intellectual grounding we need. With philosophy, we have the wisdom we need. With mindfulness, we have the tools we need to see for ourselves how our minds are giving rise to our experiences.

Let's dive in...

Part Two

Our Financial Lives

12

Financial Freedom

"All human beings seek the happy life, but many confuse the means – for example, wealth and status – with that life itself. This misguided focus on the means to a good life makes people get further from the happy life. The really worthwhile things are the virtuous activities that make up the happy life, not the external means that may seem to produce it."

—*Epictetus*

EPICTETUS, AN ANCIENT Greek Stoic philosopher, reminds us that all human beings seek a happy life, yet so often we mistake the means – wealth, status and material success – for the life we truly desire. In the pursuit of 'financial freedom', many of us concentrate solely on accumulating money, believing that if we just reach a certain threshold, happiness and peace will follow. But this misguided focus often pulls us further away from the happiness we seek, as we become trapped in a cycle of striving, accumulating and desiring more.

When money itself becomes the goal, we end up on an endless treadmill, pursuing an abstract ideal that is, by its very nature, unattainable. Financial freedom, as most imagine it, becomes a moving target: as soon as we achieve one goal, we immediately set another, convinced that just a little more will finally bring the peace we crave. But, as Epictetus suggests, the things that we pursue externally are merely tools. It's not wealth or status that leads to a good life, but rather the actions, values and virtues that we cultivate along the way.

True financial freedom, then, is not about amassing a certain amount of money but about aligning our financial decisions with what is truly important to us. It's about freeing ourselves from the obsessive focus on wealth and redirecting our energy towards living a life of meaning, purpose and virtue. When we recognise money as a means rather than an end, we can approach it with a sense of balance. We can see it as a tool to support the life we want to live, rather than as the source of that life itself.

In working with clients, I've seen first-hand how easy it is for people to become lost in the pursuit of financial security, thinking that this alone will bring happiness. Yet when they take the time to reflect on their deeper desires and what they truly value, they often realise that financial freedom is not about having more but about living well with what they have. By focusing on the 'virtuous activities' that Epictetus speaks of – building meaningful relationships, cultivating passions, contributing to others – they discover a sense of fulfilment that money alone can't provide.

Sometimes, it's certainly the case that, to live the life they truly want for themselves, people do not have enough financial resources available to them and need more to achieve these goals.

However, Epictetus' wisdom in this sense still holds true. You can be at peace and comfort with what you have, even if you still have work to do to get you to where you want to be. The journey, challenges and planning can still be fulfilling, as long as you understand that the goal is not the money but rather the purpose that the money will serve when you get there. This will alleviate the burden of 'not being there' and help you shift to a position of enjoying the challenge along the way and making incremental progress. Such a position is much more grounded and liberating than deferring your comfort until an external outcome is achieved.

As you read through the rest of this chapter, I invite you to consider what financial freedom truly means to you. Instead of focusing solely on the numbers, think about what you're really seeking. What kind of life do you want to lead? How can money serve that purpose, rather than dictate it? This shift in perspective is the first step towards a more profound sense of freedom – one rooted in purpose, not possessions or arbitrary numbers.

If money is the goal itself, then logically, it is impossible ever to satisfy the notion of financial freedom. If your goal is money, all you will be thinking about is money and you'll never be financially free (or otherwise). It's a never-ending, self-perpetuating cycle – unless you figure out what it is you're actually looking for and ultimately how money might serve that purpose. I have worked with countless individuals and families on this very idea. When you first meet them, they say that they want to be free from the shackles of money; but when you dig down into that question, they have no real idea of what 'financial freedom' actually means to them. After much deliberation, they often discover that they just don't really want to think about money as much as they do.

They just want to feel okay. Are you really going to leave your 'okayness' to an external mechanism that can change with the wind? Tax rates, borrowing rates, economic cycles, global wars and periods of sickness are all mostly out of your control, and aligning your freedom to such events is going to take your sense of comfort along for the ride.

As you may have already realised, when you are striving for financial freedom, what you are really striving for is freedom of mind and internal peace. After all, your life, thoughts, feelings and experiences are created by you and your perception of them. So how can the idea or the experience of freedom come from anywhere other than yourself? *You can be free anyway.*

Think about this: have you ever reached any of your financial goals only to realise that the feeling of security that you'd hoped would result never actually arrived or was only very fleeting? Have you ever told yourself: 'I'll feel much more at peace when…', only for that day to come and the goalposts to move suddenly? This, in itself, is evidence that attaching your comfort to external notions is unobtainable.

This is not to say that you should never think about money, or that you don't need it. It's the quality of your thinking around money that is the crux of the matter. Money is necessary for a good life in the Western world. Creating wealth is a great way to improve living standards, experiences and options in your life. It should certainly be taken seriously and treated with respect. This, however, is very different from aligning money with your sense of freedom and peace. Rather than seeing money as the goal and the deliverer of freedom, you should look at it the other way around. *From a point of internal peace and freedom, your relationship with money will be healthier and, as a by-product, your financial life can improve.*

A great real-world example of this is Julie R, a client of mine. We work closely together on her finances, asking the big questions about what it is she actually wants her life to look like. She was the headteacher of two large schools, earning a good salary with attractive pension benefits, yet she felt a slave to her salary because she 'had to' keep earning as much money as she did until she reached pension age and could retire. She felt stressed and trapped because she wanted to pursue her passions: travel, coaching people and working to her own schedule. This felt like a pipedream to her because she was working flat out and was 12 years away from being able to retire.

The life Julie wanted for herself didn't require all the money she was earning. She didn't want the boat in the harbour or first-class travel, but simply to know that she could spend some time in her life being in control of her days and having creative licence to explore her own passions. At first, she was worried that this wouldn't be possible because she had become accustomed to thinking that working for her monthly salary and protecting her earnings level were what offered her security.

But after unpicking her needs, lifestyle and expenditure, it was quite apparent that Julie had already built up enough to sustain this lifestyle; all she needed to do was earn enough to cover her expenditure until retirement without building up any further provisions. This allowed Julie to start reducing her hours in teaching while starting up her own business part time. After a year, she was earning enough from her passions to be able to give up teaching completely and she is now enjoying security of income and a protected retirement plan, all while meeting her ongoing expenditure needs with ample headroom. She is earning less than she was before, but she quickly discovered that she didn't need her higher wage in the first place and could have made the changes sooner.

Julie's thoughts changed and because of this, so did her experience. Her shift in thinking and embracement of detachment liberated her – she was finally free. She had achieved financial freedom while still working, because this was an internal challenge rather than an external one. Here, the external experience was brought into being from the inside out.

The simple shift in mindset from external to internal control allowed Julie to look at her situation with more ownership of her life structure and a disengagement from the power of money (while still treating it with the utmost respect). This is just one example of how a more considered approach can bring someone back in control of their self, with money being the tool to accomplish this, rather than their life trajectory being a servant to the money.

From this point of freedom, you can calmly evaluate what your financial goals truly are – whether that means retirement, a career change, a business acquisition or the removal of excessive debt in your life. Your ability to plan for these things and strategise how to achieve them is so much greater when you are doing this free of any emotional burden or attachment and have stopped aligning your sense of well-being to whether or not the financial outcome will be achieved.

Here's a healthier way of approaching this:

- Ask yourself what you want your life to look like. ('What will I be doing? Where will I be working? What projects will I be working on, and where?')
- Think about how to achieve this and the steps needed to get there.
- Figure out how much money it will require and the income you'll need.
- Decide where you are now in relation to this.
- Remind yourself that you can still enjoy the process of getting there (if you aren't already) because your sense of well-being isn't waiting on the other side but is already there for the taking, if you want it.
- Go out and get it! This will be much easier from a positive mental position than through struggle alone.

If that isn't enough, let me end this chapter with a story of when I met one of my wealthiest clients – a top London executive with a lot more money than most of us could ever dream of. He was hoping to retire after a long, hard, stressful and very well-paid career. He had millions in liquid assets at his disposal. When we met, he was a bit taken aback when my first question to him as soon as we had finished the pleasantries was, "So, what makes you tick?" He had never given this much thought; but ultimately, without knowing the answer to this, how could he answer his question of whether he could retire or not? If it was yachts and mansions that he wanted, the answer could be entirely different than if he wanted to spend his days birdwatching.

His answer? The things he valued most in life were nature, walking, expanding his mind, good food, reading and exercising. Only one of these things costs money.

It was at this moment that it dawned on him where his true wealth was – and that he'd had it his entire life without realising it. There we were: a multimillionaire and his financial planner, laughing in a glass-fronted office in central London about how we'd been duped by our own thought patterns!

Go out and make things happen; strive, save, invest and do meaningful work. But do so knowing what really matters to you.

13

A Peaceful Path to, and Through, Your Child's Education

"Attachment is the root of suffering."

—*The Buddha*

A CORE PRINCIPLE OF Buddhism is that our attachment to external factors such as desire, comparison or jealousy leads to great unnecessary suffering – that is, letting our egos influence our well-being. Many decisions that we make and experiences that we have in our financial lives are forged through attachment. We feel that our purchases and financial decisions have some sort of external validation, influenced by how we may be perceived out in the world.

In financial matters, we frequently attach our self-worth to external symbols – whether it's the school our children attend, the homes we live in or the cars we drive. We may feel pressure to make financial choices that are rooted not in necessity or personal values but rather in how we want to be perceived by others. This attachment to external validation can create a cycle of suffering because our financial decisions are being driven by societal comparisons, envy or a fear of judgement rather than a clear sense of what truly matters for ourselves and our families.

For example, when deciding whether to send your child to a private or state school, the influence of this attachment can be profound. You may feel that sending your child to a prestigious private school will reflect positively on you or elevate your family's social status. However, this decision, if made primarily to appease external perceptions, can come with significant financial strain or even compromise other important aspects of your well-being or your child's education. In contrast, choosing a state school may prompt feelings of inferiority or jealousy when you see other families opting for expensive private education. Both reactions stem from the same place: attachment to how you are perceived by the world, rather than what truly serves your child and your family.

This is where the Buddha's wisdom comes into play. Detachment doesn't mean indifference or neglecting important decisions. Instead, it's about freeing yourself from the grasp of ego-driven desires and external pressures. By letting go of attachment, you create space for clearer, more thoughtful decision-making. This allows you to choose from a place of authenticity, considering what aligns with your values, your family's needs and your financial reality – not from a place of comparison or fear of judgement. Observing the inner workings of your mind can help you see where this comes from and this is the first step in working to change that habitual thinking.

Where you send your children to school is often a difficult choice for many parents. Locality, resources, reputation and rankings are obvious factors that you need to consider before committing your children to a large and very influential stage of their lives.

Another big choice that many people deliberate over is whether to send their children to private school or state school. There is no right or wrong answer here and you have your own choices to make. The premise of this chapter is to explore where this thinking actually comes from and ensure that when you do make this decision, it is done from a considered position rather than an attachment to some external perspective.

Some of you will likely be reading this and thinking, 'I don't have these choices – if only!' Great – that's one thing off your plate; but there is still plenty to learn from this issue.

School parent culture can be pretty toxic. It's not just the private versus state school debate either. The comparisons at the school gate or in the parent WhatsApp groups are just as, if not more, problematic.

And the judgement goes both ways: state school parents are judging private school parents and private school parents are judging state school parents. The truth here is that this exchange of energy is exactly the same thing – it's unhelpful thinking about something out there in the world that is, in truth, neither good nor bad. We all have different inside-out driven realities.

We facilitate our feelings on such matters through our egos and how we feel our school choice reflects on us among our peers. The fact that everyone thinks their position is the right one is all the evidence you'll ever need that you're conjuring up these experiences all on your own.

Many parents put themselves under significant financial pressure to pay for private school at the expense of other things – and for all the wrong reasons. Many others who could easily afford it don't do it, even if it's right for their child. The key is to approach the issue with clarity and non-judgement to allow for a better, more appropriate decision-making experience.

Too much attachment to money (and what it 'says about you') may make you either send your kids to private school when you can't afford to or be so attached to hoarding your money and its power that you don't do it, even if it's the best option for your child's specific needs. Of course, for many people, paying for schooling is not a viable option at all; but being disgusted at those who do indicates an unhelpful attachment to money and social status. Some part of your well-being is disrupted by the family next door who have sent their children to private school. Likewise, getting some odd satisfaction from being able to pay for school fees when your neighbour can't (or chooses not to) is another example of this money-mind intrusion – they are two sides of the same coin.

When approaching financial decisions around education (or any other investments, for that matter), it's important to remember some basic facts:

- You have no idea how much pressure some people are under to send their children to private school or whether in fact it is the right thing for them or their children.
- The fact that other kids are educated privately has no influence on your feelings about your own child's path, unless you yourself create those feelings through your own thoughts.
- If you think others are judging you because they sent their kids to private school, that has nothing to do with you.

They may actually be envious of you for not having all the additional financial responsibilities! Even if they are judging you, it still has absolutely nothing to do with you; they're just having their own thought-felt experiences.

- It is also very true the other way around. Those who choose to stay in the state school system, even if they could easily afford to go private, may choose not to for their own reasons. The lesson here is that you really have no idea what anyone's circumstances are and it's much easier not to bother thinking about it – or at least to notice that you're having these thoughts.
- Societal pressures and comparisons can lead to very poor decision-making if left unchecked. The manifestations over who is doing what can influence the decisions you make for your own children on completely irrational grounds that are very rarely accurate because the only reality you truly understand is your own. Even then, that can't be fully trusted as some universal truth, as your mind is simply a prediction engine attempting to make sense of the world. Understanding this brings humility.

A helpful way to approach decisions about your child's education could encompass the following questions:

- 'What is the real reason I want my child to go to this state or private school?'
- 'If private school is best, is there enough budget to afford it?'
- 'What would I have to give up to make it happen?'
- 'What is the opportunity cost of this endeavour versus what else I could do with the money (e.g., savings or investments for the child's future)?'

- "What are my child's needs? What benefits could they get from this choice?"
- "Is a broad and more diverse pupil demographic important to me?"
- "What are the travel and cost considerations?"
- "What are our values and does this decision align with them?"

The key is to forget about what everyone else is doing and remember that this is a decision that only concerns you and your own family!

Come back to this same process if your circumstances change. There is nothing to fear if your initial option is no longer suitable and you need to re-evaluate. Stay clear and level-headed. Access that place of wisdom, non-attachment and stillness, rather than being driven by emotional or ego-driven desires.

By adopting some spiritual philosophy and understanding the nature of your own attachments, you can spot them before they make the decision for you. This will allow you to take a step back and make a rational and reasoned choice as to what is the correct course of action given your own circumstances, without the unhelpful influence of Mr or Ms Ego.

14

Inherit with Confidence and Clarity

"Wealth is the slave of a wise man and the master of a fool."

—*Seneca*

SENECA, UNLIKE MANY Stoics in ancient Rome, was not only a wise but also a very wealthy man. While some could argue that his extreme wealth might make his philosophy seem hypocritical, I believe his teachings to be a great asset when it comes to the world of money. Seneca's work, particularly the quote above, is especially pertinent to the entire premise of this book. Money in and of itself doesn't mean anything until you give it meaning. A reasoned mind, guided by wisdom and logic, is the master of money rather than its slave. You can consume or save it to benefit your life and those around you; or you can let it consume you through attachment, obsession and sentiment.

Inheriting money is a perfect example of this. A key trend I have witnessed, due to demographic changes, is the passing of the baby boomer generation who leave, or are due to leave, significant sums to the next generation. The same issues come up constantly that can often get in the way.

Before you receive an inheritance, no matter how large or small, you may think it will bring you options, freedom and security. However, it's often the case that individuals and families, upon receipt of an inheritance, become overburdened by responsibility, principle, duty and panic.

Meet Mr O, a person who has just inherited a significant (to him – again, what is and isn't significant is entirely subjective) amount of money. When he knew it was coming, he was looking forward to getting his affairs in order and setting himself up for the future. He found, however, that once the money had landed in his bank account, he was awash with panic about the meaning he ought to give it. He didn't regard it as money he had 'earned' and, in fact, could never see it as 'his' at all. He would say things like: "If I'd earned this money myself, I would do all the usual things I should be doing, but I want to keep this money separate and safe."

Mr O wasn't prepared to invest his inheritance because he felt putting it at risk would undermine his respect for the legacy. Again, this was just a concept conjured up by his own mind rather than the reality. Ironically, the money he was left had been invested for 50 years before he received it, and he only had it in the first place because it had benefitted from long-term growth by being rationally and sensibly invested. If his late family member had felt the same way about their money in the first place, Mr O would have inherited much less.

This is quite clearly a case of a thought-felt experience and an apparent overattachment to the emotional powers of money hampering or interfering with the rational decisions that need to be made. Inherited money is no different from the money that you receive in your pay cheque: it's all just money. This is not to say that squandering an inheritance is in any way the right thing to do; rather, that you should view an inheritance with as much rationality and respect as you would your other money. If you're overspending your earnings and getting into unhelpful debt, but you won't touch your inheritance, you are negatively impacting your overall financial position simply because your thoughts are telling you that the two are separate entities. But they are not: they all form part of your overall financial situation. This, in behavioural economics terms, is called 'mental accounting' and it is widely known to have the potential for detrimental results.

Mr O didn't need the money to have meaning. He needed to give it meaning. Eventually, he used the funds to secure his family's future and shore up potential university costs or house deposits for his children – which is plenty of meaning, if you ask me. He also realised that he was viewing his own money and his inherited money irrationally, and he started giving meaning to his earned income in a much better way too.

The same theory applies to all the different 'pots' of money that you have, not just an inheritance. There is only 'one' money, and that's the amount that you have or don't have.

The only thing that differs between an inheritance and your personal income or savings is your thinking around them. Money from a legacy is merely a figure in your account and your approach to decision-making around it should be no different just because of where it has come from; to treat it otherwise means that your mind and your thoughts are ruling the roost. You would be leaving your wellness on the table.

A helpful way to consider any windfall such as an inheritance is to think of it as no different from any other money (since it is exactly the same thing). For completeness, however, let's consider a few questions to ask yourself if you receive an inheritance:

- 'What are my long-term financial goals?'
- 'How will this money interplay with these objectives?'
- 'Do I need the money in the short term?'
- 'Do I have any high-interest debts that I can clear?'
- 'Do I want to leave a legacy for my own children? Is there enough for that?'
- 'Are any tax breaks available to me that I can utilise?'
- 'Can I lock it away for a while?'
- 'How can I invest this money for the future?'
- 'Do I need to make this decision now?'

Remind yourself that money in itself is simply a concept in the outside world. Your anxieties and worries about it, or what should be done with it, are simply created by your thoughts *about* the money. You do not need to change your thinking about money *per se* but simply understand where such thinking comes from and how it manifests. With that, you can look at things a bit more objectively and make the appropriate decisions.

Remember: in the first weeks and months after you've inherited money, you may not be in the best place to deal with these decisions – and that's okay too. Think of an inheritance the same way you would approach any other financial decision, giving detached and reasoned consideration to how this tool can serve your objectives. An inheritance is a final gift from your loved ones to provide you with further security and options; it was never intended to create debilitating attachment.

15

How to Get Clarity on Debt

"A wise person avoids extremes, excesses and complacency."

—*Lao Tzu*

TAOISM, AN ANCIENT Chinese philosophy championed by Lao Tzu in around 500 BCE, is focused on a balanced and centred approach to life. You will likely be familiar with and know the meaning of the yin-yang, a core symbol of Taoism. This symbol reflects the dualisms and dichotomies in the world (e.g., good and evil; male and female). The underlying meaning of this is that all forces of nature and of our being are balanced and harmonious.

This concept can be applied to our relationship with money and the subject of this chapter: how we work with debt. The extremes on both sides of the debate, which we will explore here, can be problematic if the harmonious balance is interrupted. However, it is possible to be centred and rational when working with debt, as long as we do so from a position of logic and detachment. The Stoics would argue for a reasoned choice around debt rather than an emotional one. Buddhists would argue for decision-making around debt to be detached and not predicated on some arbitrary attachment that you wrongly think is shaping your well-being. A Taoist, as we have explored, would argue that debt is neither good nor bad and works in balance with other opposing forces, such as extreme complacency. A certain level of debt can be used to encourage growth at the right time, whereas debt can be too burdensome if carried to excess. All these philosophies complement each other and bring us back to the central point about the importance of making financial decisions from a place of tranquillity and peace, rather than fear, greed or status.

Debt is an interesting phenomenon. Some of us can be so overburdened by fear of it that we don't utilise it properly for our own good. It also has the opposite effect on some of us, in that we get so seduced by the power of 'now' that we accumulate too much debt in a problematic way that hinders our experience of life.

All of the money books will tell you that there is good debt and bad debt. An example of good debt is where the debt is used to leverage your position and create returns for you over and above the cost of the debt. Of course, there are calculated risks involved in the decision-making process, but at least they are – well, calculated. Purchasing a house, for example, gets most people into very significant debt that can take between one-third and one-half of their adult life to service. However, most would argue that this is a very worthwhile debt to take on and that their lives are the better for it. Of course, this is not a risk-free move, as the value of a house can change, whereas the debt – and your interest on it – remains fixed.

An example of bad debt is your stereotypical overspender, accumulating credit card debt or loans to buy shoes, cars, restaurant meals and experiences that their budget simply doesn't allow for. This creates a spiral of accrued interest at significant rates over time that can have a negative impact on the lives of those affected. It seldom leads to happiness. I liken this to my own historic indulgences: a temporary reprieve with no long-term mental security.

However, there are those who avoid debt at all costs and to their own detriment. A good example of this is the business owner with a fantastic opportunity who is simply unwilling to get into debt as a matter of principle and misses the opportunity as a result. Another example is the family who want – and thoroughly deserve – a hard-earned holiday but are not prepared to put it on a 0% credit card even though they would easily clear the debt with a few month's wages and a sensible, pragmatic approach.

The fundamental reality here, as I've argued consistently throughout this book, is that the reality of debt is created from the inside out, entirely by your own thought. Debt is neither good nor bad; it is just debt. It is a tool that you can use either to your benefit or to your detriment. It's how your thought-felt experience produces your own interactions with debt that is of paramount importance. As I have said before, we do ultimately have some control over this: all we have to do is observe these manifestations from an impartial position.

Racking up excessive credit card fees due to overspending is evidence of an unhealthy relationship with money. For such people, their well-being is too closely associated with the material world, causing them problems. Under the same principle, the business owner who is afraid of debt is missing a potentially worthwhile opportunity because their outside-in understanding of debt has led to thoughts of negativity and fear, meaning that their lost opportunity is taken up by someone else. As we have already learned, this is not how your experiences are shaped. You create them. Your mind and, by extension, your thoughts create the experience of the stimuli you are responding to. With this understanding, you can look at your relationship with debt in a more pragmatic and distanced way.

Here are some healthy questions about taking on debt that you can ask yourself from this position of clarity:

- 'What are the pros and cons of my decision?'
- 'How will it improve/diminish my overall financial position?'
- 'Am I really buying this item for me or am I buying it for my ego or to prove my worth to others?'
- 'Can I afford it? Will the repayments be problematic for me in the future?'
- 'What is the opportunity cost for me later in life of doing it or not doing it?'
- 'Will I be thankful that I did this in one, two, five or ten years' time?'
- 'Will I regret not doing it?'

If you consider these points carefully, you can make the decision with much greater clarity and then move on with your life! Remember: there is nothing to be gained from deliberating over your choice after the fact; though you should check in every so often and see where you stand with it and whether any changes are needed (if they can be made).

By approaching debt from a place of clarity, detachment and balance, we can regain control over our financial lives. Rather than fear or overindulgence, we can make debt work for us – just as any tool should be used, with wisdom and care. We can apply this same wisdom when we are debating whether to pay off debt or explore investment/business opportunities. Take the emotive influence out of the equation and ask the rational question: 'What is the optimum course of action for my circumstances and goals?'

16

Free Yourself from the Financial Media

"Risk comes from not knowing what you're doing."

—*Warren Buffett*

WARREN BUFFETT IS one of the most successful investors of all time. But, aside from his fortune made through successful investing, what is equally striking about him is that he is admirably tranquil, wise and grounded. He is a great example of how to operate and utilise the monetary system in an effective way without letting it inform your view of what makes life worth living. Buffett applies a logical, rational approach to his investment decisions and lives a very normal life without being overburdened by ego and material influences. He also communicates with much less hysteria than you will often find in media outlets the world over when it comes to talking about money. We should look to Buffett's wisdom and pragmatism during the inevitable financial frenzies that the world finds itself in from time to time.

We all intrinsically understand that the media, financial or otherwise, can affect how we view the world. The financial press, economists' projections and social media all report on the world of money with great fanfare, so it is very important when reading them to check in with your mind's internal appraisal and how this plays out on your own projection or experience.

An outside-in view of the world (which we now know isn't how things really work) would view a news story simply as something that informs our thoughts, which then create our feelings. However, the reality is that the mind projects its own thinking from the sensory input it receives and then guesses what is out there. Why is this so fundamentally different? When a news story says, 'Stock market loses £100 billion in value in a day,' it's very easy to think that, as this story is negative in nature, your thoughts and feelings about it must also be negative, because the story (or the 'outside') directly informs your well-being and interpretation of the matter. The real truth is that you receive sensory input and your mind attempts to make sense of it. Your mind makes it either negative, neutral or positive. This is why, particularly with money, we all respond so differently to exactly the same thing.

This has led, and continues to lead, to some highly negative consequences when people see things from the outside in (rather than creating their own experience from the inside out). It can result in poor decisions – for example, selling investments at the wrong time due to acting through feelings and emotions rather than rationally.

I couldn't count the number of times I have received panic emails and calls in response to news headlines. One of the many great pleasures of being a financial adviser is that before any reckless or emotionally driven decisions take place, I can prevent them from happening. This is achieved by interrupting the experience that is about to manifest itself into reality through troubled thinking. The truth is that the power to do this yourself is firmly within your control. There is an impermanence to everything in our universe, including the financial media's narrative of what is going on. Outsourcing any sense of your comfort to it will never be helpful.

The news very rarely has a headline the following week saying, '£100 billion added back onto stock market value in just a few days.' Bad news sells, as we all know; so, it's up to us to approach world events with a sense of consideration and pragmatism in order to regain control.

In the emotionally fuelled world of money, it is absolutely imperative to understand how your thoughts about these events come about. Reading a headline and taking any sort of action from a point of hysteria, excitement, fear or greed is rarely a good financial move. If you catch yourself acting through emotion, notice that is the case, wait for it to pass and then approach the situation and determine whether any action is required.

As a financial adviser, I have encountered a number of clients who communicate with me within about 30 minutes of a news outbreak, often panicking about a global event and how it may affect their financial position. When this happens, it's obvious that they are acting in this way due to an emotionally charged response rather than from a clear and calm perspective. In these instances, you need to understand that the news has come in and that you yourself have then created your experience of it through your thoughts and feelings, generating a negative position which you are then acting from. Noticing this is a profound deviation from what you might normally do because you consciously watch it manifesting and unfolding before you. Once caught, you can reset, take some time and wait for a clearer headspace. Thoughts, as we have learned, arise moment to moment and are impermanent (just like everything else). This helps you to regain some control over your mind and, therefore, your experiences out there in the world.

A striking example of this is when the Covid-19 lockdown was first announced in March 2020. The media and global stock markets went into a frenzy and the markets' value was temporarily reduced – in some cases by as much as 30%. The media reported this, of course, and many people sold out of their investment portfolios with significant – sometimes life-changing – losses. The truth is that such seismic events have happened a number of times throughout history and the markets have always gone on to recover. In this particular case, within a matter of months, they were back to exactly where they had been before lockdown was announced.

So, what was it that made these people lose so much money in 2020? Was it the stock market or their own thought-driven fear? The people who remained calm and collected were able to take a step back and ride out the storm – and are far better off today as a result. This is evidence that the 'event' itself did not cause the negative result; instead, the individuals themselves created the experience through their thoughts. Such attachment to well-being and temporary monetary value can be financially disastrous. Buddhist and Stoic teachings discuss loosening attachment as a core principle for a more peaceful existence. Without attachment in this case, not only would you have a more tranquil experience but, by not being attached to market fluctuations, you'd have less financial hardship too. It's a win-win.

It's important to keep abreast of financial news to ensure that you have the appropriate information to make decisions. The key thing to remember here is that having a better understanding of how your mind generates your feelings about events will enable you to take a step back: you will know that your well-being is intact despite the chaos in the outside world. From this point of clarity, your financial decision-making will be profoundly better.

When the media is in a frenzy over financial matters, here are a few questions that you can ask yourself:

- 'How does this impact the life I am living right now?'
- 'Do I have time on my side to wait things out?'
- 'What historically has happened after major financial events?'
- 'What changes should I make, if any, in light of this news?'
- 'Has anything fundamentally changed in my financial/life plan?'
- 'Do I need to make any adjustments to ensure that I stay on track in light of this development?'
- 'Am I being driven by my emotions, fears or excitement here? Should I wait to make this decision?'
- 'Is now the right time to make such a decision?'

Remember, it's not the financial uncertainty but your thoughts about it that are disturbing you. Detach, allow the emotional response to pass and consider things again when you are thinking more clearly. Your inner space can be calm despite the outside noise. Your journey will also be calm as a result of this clarity.

17

Elevate Your Future and Enjoy Today with Ease

"He who knows that enough is enough will always have enough."

—*Lao Tzu*

ANCIENT CHINESE PHILOSOPHER Lao Tzu had a lot to say about being content and balanced. Here, he states that the idea of 'enough' is paramount to internal well-being. Attachment comes in many forms and manifests itself in different ways, but ultimately the result is the same. Attachment to outside influences, particularly money, disturbs your internal equilibrium. Attachment detracts us from what we know about the mind and how experiences are truly formed.

One area of your finances that a problematic relationship with money can hamper the most is saving and investing for your future. The interference of 'now' and an aversion to risk can have dramatic implications for this. On the other hand, over-prioritising future saving out of financial fear can impact the life that you live now. There are those who recklessly give little respect to their future situation and those who have such an attachment to holding onto their money that they forget to use it as what it is: a tool. Money is energy. Very few strike the right balance, and I believe that a lot of this behaviour can be explained by the mechanics of the mind. A freer, more pragmatic mind, devoid of attachment, may well be the answer to finding some harmony between protecting your future financial position and not causing friction to how you live your life today.

Mr and Mrs C are a married couple who have scrimped and saved and lived very modestly all their lives. They finally retired a couple of years ago and have amassed a large sum which they are not spending. They have the ability to finance a lifestyle many multiples above their current expenditure, but they haven't touched a penny of their investments and savings despite having a long list of things they want to do (travel, home renovations, social experiences). When asked why they haven't yet done any of these things, they explain that, as working-class people, they have been conditioned to spend very little and they simply can't bring themselves to reduce the balance of their savings in order to live their lives more fully and purposefully. It would upset them to see the number on the screen become slightly smaller, despite the overwhelmingly positive experiences that they could have with the financial tools available to them.

Can you see here that their attachments have controlled their experiences through life and even into retirement? This is further proof that any notion of externally provided freedom is a myth. Money is a wonderful energy, but it can't give you freedom unless you make it so.

On the other hand, Ms W – a high earner with over £175,000 of annual income – has thousands spare after each pay cheque and manages to spend every last penny. The money usually goes on meals out, holidays and new cars, with the focus very much on immediate consumption, while completely ignoring future expenditure needs. When asked why even a small amount couldn't be put away for the future, her answers frequently involve sentiments such as, "Life is for living now" and "I could get hit by a bus or get sick tomorrow." While these outcomes are of course possible, they are also unlikely. What is certain is that the ability to sustain such a lifestyle in the future is impossible without future provision. Ms W will get a shock when there is a stark change to how she lives in the future because she has put nothing aside to mitigate this.

What is lacking in each of these two cases is balance. Though they are at opposite ends of the spectrum, these two scenarios are equally problematic. Mr and Mrs C have let their thoughts about reducing their savings create a reality where anything less than what they have now would ultimately be a terrible thing. Money – or indeed, the amount of it – as an outside concept has informed their sense of well-being, and they feel that the number needs to be the same or higher for their comfort to remain intact. An understanding that this is a thought-felt projection that they themselves have created will hopefully allow them to change course and start to do something meaningful with the money that they have worked hard for and saved in a sensible and planned way. The truth is that they could have had a more balanced life both while they were working and now in retirement.

On the other hand, Ms W has attached too much of her sense of well-being to 'here and now' consumption, to the detriment of a future which is, statistically, very likely to arrive. This is still an attachment to money, but in the opposite sense. An understanding that the mind, and thus the mind's wellness, is an inside-out process rather than being formed in the outside world might just help her to disassociate her wellness from excessive consumption sufficiently to be able to make some future provision. This will still allow her to enjoy her life plentifully now, but also safeguard the future her, who will likely thank the present her for this consideration. While it's true that all we have is the present moment, one thing that is almost certain is that there will be other present moments to come for us, and providing tools for these moments too seems sensible and balanced. I am pleased that she is now doing this and slowly realising that her life is just as enjoyable and wholesome as it was before. I'm still working on Mr and Mrs C…!

Both of these are examples of greed and attachment: greed for immediate consumption or greed for accumulation without being able to let go. As the ancient Chinese yin-yang symbol tells us, there is a harmonious balance to be found between these two extremes.

The message here is that you need to think and plan for your future, but you don't need to deliberate over it constantly. Understanding your mind and seeing that money is simply an external concept should help to loosen the grip it has on your attitude towards future saving (in both the over- and under-prioritised sense). From this place, we can begin to let go of these attachments and allow ourselves to truly live.

A more considered approach to future saving is to say to yourself, 'Okay, this is something I need to do but in a balanced and sensible way.' Detaching your well-being from your financial position or consumption tendencies will allow you to understand that you will be okay if you buy less stuff (so you can protect your future self); or indeed, that you will be okay if you spend some of your money!

Some questions to ask yourself if you're planning for the future could include the following:

- 'What do I want to be doing in the future? How much will this realistically cost?'
- 'How much and for how long do I need to save regularly to achieve this?'
- 'How much risk am I happy to take and what are the risks involved with planning for this?'
- 'How comfortable am I with fluctuating values?' (Don't forget the theory!)
- 'What is a sensible budget for my life right now, considering that my sense of "okayness" is not attached to consumption?'
- 'What can I lock away for a while?'
- 'What growth can I expect on my money and are there any tax reliefs available to me to bolster this?'
- 'Where is a good place to put my money to achieve my objectives?'
- 'Will this plan lead me to over-saving or under-saving, or will it be about right?'

If you find yourself struggling to utilise the money that you have saved, you could ask yourself the following questions:

- 'Do I realistically need all these savings?'
- 'What have I always wanted to do? Is this reasonable in light of what I have available?'
- 'What is the real reason I haven't been utilising my money fully?'
- 'If I do these things, how much will I have left and how long will it last?'
- 'Could I help others and do some good with some of these funds if they're not needed?'

With these questions answered (and remember: if you're not comfortable answering them yourself, you can always get help from a qualified financial professional), you can come up with a plan, put it in place and let go of the need to deliberate over it. Moreover, you will also let go of the misconception that your well-being is informed by these outside metrics. It's important to check in from time to time to see how your plan is going and whether you're on track, but you can soon go back to living your life in the here and now without letting your moment-to-moment thoughts determine the money-mind narrative.

18

A More Conscious Approach to Risk

"You have the right to work, but never to the fruit of the work. You should never engage in action for the sake of reward, nor should you long for inaction."

—The Bhagavad Gita

THE CONCEPT OF taking risks, especially with our money, is made much easier and more logical when we understand the inside-out nature of our minds and experiences. It is also incredibly helpful to observe our relationship with money through ancient and spiritual wisdom. The above quote from a Hindu scripture reflects one of its central teachings, outlining the importance of making calculated and rational decisions, and also warning of the problems of not taking action.

Often, we approach risk-taking through emotion rather than rationality, which can lead to unhelpful action – or indeed, unhelpful inaction. It is also true that if our well-being and inner peace are tied to our finances, then our judgement is clouded and we can make poor decisions. For some, this may be taking uncalculated and reckless risks from excitement, greed and the idea that, 'If this pays off, I will be happy.' On the other hand, many people may avoid taking risks entirely as the emotional attachment to money has paralysed their ability to explore passions and interests that may be advantageous to them in the long run.

As with debt, risk is neither good nor bad but simply something to be approached pragmatically when we make decisions about what to do with our money and what may or may not serve us well. As with many things, there is also a certain risk inherent in not taking any risk at all, which we will explore together in this chapter.

When many people think of risk, they think of losing money. While this may be justified to some extent, the fear of loss is often overamplified by the thoughts that accompany it which manifest and can become problematic.

First, risk is a very subjective matter. We all have completely different understandings of risk, what it means and how we feel about it. This in itself proves that it's not really the outside world causing our experiences; rather, we ourselves create them from our own internal space and project them outwards (otherwise, we would all feel the same about taking risks).

Risk is all around us. Every step out of the door, every conversation we have, every decision we make to spend, save or invest our money has a risk attached to it. It may be the risk of loss, of being unable to pay back what we owe or of a negative effect on our financial future through not taking any risks in the first place.

There are calculated long-term risks approached from a point of clarity and logic; and then there are, of course, reckless risks fuelled by greed, excitement or frenzy. There are also people who are so fearful of loss that they don't take any 'risk' whatsoever and the compounded impact of decades-long inflation eats away at the buying power of their money. Many see the latter as risk free – but is it? Or is this acceptance of guaranteed inflationary risk simply the result of fear that there will be times when money fluctuates in saleable value? Are we really saying to ourselves that uncertainty means we are not okay?

A clear mind that understands the role of its own inside-out mechanism in the creation of experiences will look at risk in a logical way. Without an overattachment between money and well-being, a more balanced approach to fear of loss and the true cost of inaction can be achieved. Investing over the long term has been nothing short of overwhelmingly positive for financial wellness in the last 100 years, if it has been done in a sensible and diversified way. It is often our thinking around the matter that leads to poor experiences or outcomes. Detaching your well-being from the peaks and troughs of the investment cycle, I believe, is the key to benefitting from this in the long run, while also keeping your well-being intact along the way.

If you have already invested money but find yourself worrying about it or checking your portfolio value every day, you are in some way aligning your sense of comfort and peace with the monetary value of your investments. If it goes up, you feel good; if it goes down, you don't. The market value of your portfolio has likely changed while reading this sentence, so attaching any part of your comfort to this outside world mechanism over which you have no control seems rather illogical. Instead, you should let it do what it does in the knowledge that your well-being is already intact. Check in every so often to see how it aligns with the goals and plans you have made – and then, please, just get on with your life!

Outsourcing your internal comfort or security to something that you can't control, rather than working on your inner space (which you can), is illogical and destined to fail.

Why would you check your portfolio, pension and savings balances every single day to see whether you are going to be happy today or not? Put that way, doesn't it seem like madness? Or why would you leave your money in a bank rather than put it to work so you can sleep at night knowing that it will still have the same value tomorrow? This is equally problematic because you are still attaching your sense of security to a number on a screen, when the truth is that your experiences are born out of thoughts and feelings over which you do have some element of control.

For most of us, investing is a vital part of future financial planning – be it through our pension funds, property, business ventures or retirement plans. Put a plan in place and know what you are working towards, diversify sensibly, check in with it every now and again, don't over-leverage and just get on with things! When you approach risk from a more considered and balanced position, you are protecting yourself from emotionally charged decisions (fear and/or overexcitement), which are the true causes of poor outcomes – with regard both to the risk of not taking any risk and, of course, to reckless, miscalculated risks.

I will use Mr and Mrs L as an example here. They invested some of their money at the top of the market before a global inflation and cost-of-living crisis. This made the markets very volatile and, ever since, their portfolio has been recovering. Some asset classes performed particularly badly during the crisis and have been in recovery mode since then. Mr and Mrs L have often said that they will be happy when their portfolio gets back to where it was before the crisis. They have applied an arbitrary point in time, which is unknowable, when they will allow themselves to be happy and feel secure again. Despite having more money than they need and plenty of savings, which they would be unable to get through in at least five years, they are still attaching their well-being to something outside their control. We all understand rationally that financial markets rise and fall constantly but tend to increase in value over the long run. So why is it that some of us delay our sense of tranquillity until the financial markets tell us it's okay? Isn't it better just to be okay in the meantime?

The reality in the above situation is that the alternative would be to leave all the money in a bank account and lose value to inflation as a guaranteed risk for eternity. Even if a market downturn takes a while to recover from, remember: you have not engaged in investing for an emotional reward but should be making financial decisions for logical, rational and optimal reasons. Whether your financial situation is up or down, this rationality as to why you've done what you've done still holds true. It's your own inside-out reality that conjures up any sense of insecurity you may feel. Thankfully, we know by now that we can work on this to make our realities better!

Let the development of mankind over time do its work. Let go of the uncontrollable: it has no power over you. You are the crafter of your comfort. Risk is temporary; your ability to let go and be free is permanent. This is accessible to everyone right now. It just takes a bit of work; but boy, is it worth it.

19

Overcome the Fear of Scarcity

"We are not rich by what we possess but by what we can do without."

—*Immanuel Kant*

WELL-KNOWN EIGHTEENTH-CENTURY GERMAN philosopher Immanuel Kant was a key figure of the Enlightenment period. The Enlightenment was a philosophical movement that helped to pioneer the modern-day ideas of individual liberty and individual rights. It is understood to have inspired historical movements such as the American and French revolutions, shaping some of the modern and innovative republics that we see around the world today. What Kant says here is a piece of simple, effective wisdom that we can incorporate into our daily lives. When it comes to money, many people around the world – especially after the recent inflation crises – are finding it difficult to make ends meet. If we find ourselves with little, can we still be okay? Can we do with less and still be happy if the budget doesn't balance? The answer is yes, as we understand fundamentally that our well-being and our financial situation are two separate things. Of course, having more financial resources is helpful because it reduces the frequency with which we need to address our thoughts to our finances; but ultimately, in times of hardship, you can still keep your well-being intact – it may just require a little more effort than if you had no financial constraints. The reality remains the same: how you experience money is an internally generated manifestation.

Much of what we have talked about so far has concerned the psychological aspects faced by people who have money to allocate or even consider. While the understanding of the mind is applicable to all areas of financial life, what about those who are struggling to make ends meet?

It is undoubtedly easier to remember and reconcile the understanding of the mind when faced with financial decisions if you actually have money in the first place! However, the principle of how your experiences are formed is no less true when your financial position is far more difficult. It is, indeed, more challenging to remain calm, collected and considered when facing financial difficulty; but it is just as important, if not more so. The actions that you take may be different, but the fact that your experiences are formed by your thoughts and subsequently your feelings (rather than the outside 'event' in itself) is still completely true.

It is fair to say that the last few years have been difficult financially for many. A significant energy crisis, leading to a full-blown cost-of-living crisis and amplified interest rate rises, has left many people the world over struggling to make ends meet. With family budgets stretched past the point of effective reconciliation, financial panic and emotionally charged thinking are, no doubt, very intense during these times. This is completely understandable in the face of such uncertainty and hardship.

A good example can be drawn from the story of a client of mine, Ms B. Ms B was made redundant and had only a couple of months to find a new job. With a child to support, fuel to buy for her car and little savings other than in her retirement plans (which she was too young to access), she was beginning to panic. Questions bubbled up, such as: 'What am I going to do? How am I going to feed my child? What if we become homeless? What will people think? How have I failed?' Reading this, you may be familiar with such thought patterns: an external event (in this case, redundancy) triggers a thought-driven response, which creates an experience of panic. It is very easy to get this way when something seems or feels so existential. This financial challenge was indeed a difficult one. However, did panicking and asking those questions land Ms B a new job? Reduce her costs? Put food on the table? Solve the problem? I will leave these rhetorical questions unanswered…

From a calmer place, we were able to work through Ms B's budget, find unnecessary expenditures and cut them back temporarily to keep hold of some small savings and thus cushion the job search process. We explored extending her mortgage term to reduce her monthly payments and looked at how a cheaper car would help with expenditure costs. Suddenly, if necessary, there was scope for a four-month job search before further action needed to be taken: this freed up some time for Ms B to assess her options. Initially, when discussing these measures, she would respond with arguments such as, "I need to keep this" or "I can't reduce that." Ultimately, this was because there was still some attachment between her well-being and her material expenditure. Eventually, Ms B understood that even if she had to move house, sell the car, extend the mortgage and buy cheaper food, she could still be okay internally – and so could her son (who was too young to have developed material attachment anyway and, ironically, didn't care about any of it).

From this more focused and rational standpoint, Ms B was able to concentrate on refining her CV and applying for new roles. As I had expected all along, she was offered a new, better-paid job within a matter of weeks and life went back to normal. She didn't get into this new, better position because she panicked or let her internal being correlate with her hardship; she got to this point because she cleared out the noise and became comfortable with the idea of having less to begin with. She focused on what she needed to do to emerge stronger from the situation, rather than getting lost in an existential meltdown.

Ms B could have had a negative thought-generated experience that would have been unhelpful to her management of the situation she was faced with. She could also have turned it into an opportunity or a challenge to overcome, yielding completely different results. That is the power of thought and how it influences our experiences out there in the world. You can craft this more productive inner environment simply by observing it.

I understand that for some, it's harder to reduce outgoings, extend debts or search for new roles; but the principle remains the same. If you understand that your well-being and your money are not the same thing, then you can endure financial hardship more comfortably. Letting your inner peace disappear along with your money won't make you any more money – in fact, it just compounds the problem, as it means that your energy is being spent unproductively.

By thinking less emotionally about money issues (and by considering how your experiences are truly formulated), you can take a step back, observe and approach your situation with less panic. This will allow you to regain more control over how it unfolds. With a looser emotional connection to money, you may find that a lower-cost property or a cheaper car would sort out your issues. Remember: now that you are less attached to money/materialism, it won't make you any more or any less peaceful by going smaller/cheaper – that is, unless you attach your peace to it.

With this freer space, you may also gain insights that enable you to start working on that business idea you had, or to sell some stuff that's been lying around the loft for years. The time that you spend deliberating, worrying and panicking about your money troubles could be reinvested in more reasoned thinking about how you can manage or improve your situation. All of that could be achieved from a bit of mental freedom and less attachment! It takes less mental energy to do this than it does to have a thought-induced meltdown over any financial situation that you find yourself in. If this weren't enough, being anxious or uneasy over a difficult situation is not a profitable response and won't solve it; but making some space and stillness might just help you to find the solution you need to make a difference. I am not trying to give you answers here about how to get out of a financial situation; but I am trying to detach your sense of inner peace from your financial situation to allow for greater clarity to help you plan and take action yourself, from a rational and tranquil standpoint.

You'll then have the power and the tools to solve your problems on your own or to seek the appropriate help.

A reasonable approach, if you find that your budget simply isn't balancing, is to ask yourself the following questions:

- 'How many of the items in my expenditure do I really need? What can I cut out?'
- 'Can my debts be restructured?'
- 'What can I sell? What don't I truly need?' (Remember: your belongings, being outside in the material world, are not where your well-being is rooted.)
- 'Can I realistically afford to live here if there is no budget available for simple, low-cost expenditure?'
- 'How can I earn more or increase my income? What skills do I have that I can monetise?'
- 'What is the shortfall in my budget? How much extra work do I need to do at what hourly rate to plug the shortfall?'
- 'What new skills could I develop to help me grow out of this current situation?'

If a financial event or hardship presents itself to you, notice the emotions arising from it and let them pass. Understand that you can be okay with less. You can then start to think with greater ease and effectiveness about what action you can take to mitigate the situation.

20

Retire on Your Terms

"Wealth is not his that has it, but his that enjoys it."

—*Benjamin Franklin*

THIS PROFOUND STATEMENT by Franklin reminds us that wealth in itself is not the goal: its true value lies in how it enables us to enjoy life and what energy we give it. Yet for many, especially those contemplating retirement, this principle becomes difficult to embrace. Even with abundant resources, the ability to 'enjoy' wealth can be hindered by psychological barriers, deep-seated habits or a misunderstanding of what retirement truly represents.

This chapter is aimed at those who have the financial means to retire whenever they like but, for some reason, find themselves unable to take the leap. It explores the mental and emotional hurdles that keep individuals tethered to work long past the point of necessity and offers strategies to untangle these attachments. Franklin's wisdom reminds us that the accumulation of wealth is not the endgame: what matters is how we allow it to enrich our lives.

Even if you're not yet in a position to retire, it's still worth reading this chapter to help you begin to address your own retirement goals.

Retirement can be a difficult time psychologically for many people. The challenge of shifting from a growth mindset to a decumulation mindset isn't talked about enough. It requires a complete shift in how you think about your money, so it's unsurprising that this can't just be switched on and off like a light. If this is not approached correctly, some people can find it very hard to retire at all, even if they desperately want to or comfortably have the means to do so. This inability is not usually due to a lack of available funds, but rather to an overattachment to accumulation that makes it very challenging to do a complete 180 and start reducing the value of what they have saved. A money-mind detachment here could be the key to loosening the grip of this attachment so that you can find comfort and enjoyment in the descent and not just the climb. A successful mountaineer must be able to go both up the mountain and back down the mountain. They're not supposed to stay at the top once they get there!

Here are a few core reasons why those who have plenty of resources available to allow them to retire keep on working in a job that they no longer want:

- **Seeing retirement as a binary position:** Many view retirement as an all-or-nothing change of life rather than as what it truly is: an opportunity to do what you really want to (whether that's changing careers to something lower paid but more interesting, working a few days a week, starting a venture, studying, volunteering, spending more time with the family and so on).

- **Earning money is a key part of identity:** It is very common for people to associate their sense of purpose or identity with bringing a wage home; in their minds, giving this up would somehow diminish their 'worth' or sense of self. But they themselves have handed some of their identity over to this; the identity was not provided to them by it.
- **Fear of a diminishing number:** The thought of no or lower income and a reduction in savings balances can create a sense of fear and a lack of 'okayness' or safety. As a result, people may put off retirement in order to preserve well-being (in this scenario, the outside world is informing the internal well-being of the mind).
- **Attachment to income:** With a deep attachment to money as the informer of your well-being, it can be tempting to see the income that you provide or accumulate as the reason why everything is okay. This can prevent any changes from being okay.

There are, of course, many other reasons why people in this situation put off retirement (or making any changes, for that matter); but these are some of the important ones, particularly when the mind is doing its work. The simple truth is that all of these reasons can be explained, at least in part, by a misunderstanding of how your experiences are formed. The outside-in approach has you believing that these factors are things that are influencing your peace and your actions (or lack thereof). The truth, as we have learned, is that your thoughts and feelings are created in the mind and subsequently create your experiences. This simple yet profound realisation may help take the edge off just enough to see the situation for what it really is and help you decide whether you truly want to, and can, retire or not.

A diminishing number on a screen is just a diminishing number on a screen. If you have a plan in place and are keeping track of it, and the numbers still work out, then it is simply a number. How you choose to think about this is what makes it good or bad, not the number. The same goes for the sense of identity that you derive from your work: you are the one crafting your sense of identity from it, not the work itself. With this simple realisation, you may create a little space to approach things more objectively. Ask yourself the following questions:

- 'Do I still *genuinely* enjoy my work?'
- 'Why am I *really* still doing it?'
- 'Is there anything I'd rather be doing that is realistic?'
- 'What do we have saved/invested and will this sustain me/us?'
- 'What is putting me off? What am I worried about?'
- 'What do I want life to look like and what resources are required to achieve this? Do I have them already?'
- 'Is my money structured in the most effective way to make this happen? What changes could I make to optimise matters?'
- 'What do I want this next stage of my life to look like? What makes me tick?'

It's okay if you can't answer some of these questions. There are qualified professionals out there who do exactly this sort of thing for a living whom you can approach for a financial plan to see how everything stacks up. Even if it turns out that retirement or a career shift right now is unrealistic, you'll at least know how you are faring and what you need to do to make your hopes a reality. And understanding the nature of your experiences and your mental relationship with money may help you to be more at peace while you continue to work for a little while longer.

Play around with it; don't run from it! Burying your head in the sand and delaying planning your retirement is taking time away from you that you could be repurposing or aligning with your true values. That's what money does for us – and it's great at it. Let's not forget that part.

21

Create Some Distance from the Joneses

> "It is not the man who has too little, but the man who craves more, that is poor."
>
> —*Seneca*

WE HAVE ALREADY heard from Seneca in an earlier chapter, so he doesn't need further introduction. What is beautiful about this quote is the direct appeal it makes to craving or, as Buddhists would call it, desire. There is a fundamental difference between genuine aspiration to improve your financial situation and *needing* it to make you feel okay. Working towards a goal and achieving it is one thing; needing it to satisfy your sense of self-worth or inner happiness is entirely different. This leads us to an issue that we are all familiar with: keeping up with the Joneses.

Oh, Mr and Mrs Jones, how we love to keep up with you! This old adage has so much more to it than simply wanting to show ourselves as being on a level playing field with our neighbours.

It embodies our mentality around 'success' – meaning security, materialism, self-worth and, last but certainly not least, ego.

The truth of the matter is that when we compare ourselves to others – be that through our houses, our belongings, our choice of schools, our cars or otherwise – we are simply trying to find peace with our own position and satisfy our egos that are chattering away at us. By now, we should all know that our psychological well-being and ease cannot, and will not, come from the fleeting sense of satisfaction that we feel when we park a shiny new car on the drive simply to keep up with those around us. The Joneses will very shortly buy a new one to keep up with *you* and then – guess what? – you're back in the self-perpetuating cycle of disappointment and deep feelings of insignificance that you yet again need to try to satisfy. Ever wondered why the satisfaction you get from these endeavours doesn't last very long? That's because it's a lie, and it never has been – and never will be – the way to find contentment and peace. It is one of the best examples of the outside-in myth that you will ever come across. There is no internal security to be gained from external endeavours.

Of course, the introduction of the social media echo chamber has made this problem even more profound. We're no longer limited to Mr and Mrs Jones next door but can now compare ourselves to almost every single human being on the planet. Social media posts are great at showing you the highlights of everybody else's life, but they rarely show the struggles that people face on a daily basis. The same is true in real life with your neighbours, parents at school, colleagues, members of your community and even friends and family. You may never possibly know how good or bad someone else has it. The easiest, simplest and most peaceful way to address this is simply not to bother entertaining this impossible-to-satisfy merry-go-round. Sure, get yourself a shiny new car or watch, or go on a world cruise, if you truly want to and can afford it; but make sure that is the real reason you're doing it, rather than to satisfy your own ego or sense of peace. The ego is the part of the mind nattering away at you, craving attention. Put it back in its place.

Sometimes when I'm approached for financial advice, a number of clients say things like: 'I'm probably not anywhere near as rich as some of your other clients,' or 'What do other people do?' This is a great example of how people compare their financial situation to that of others in order to try to assess how secure and safe they are, without any further context on those others. Some of the most financially secure people have much smaller sums in nominal terms but, relative to their needs, what they have is more than ample. Some with far greater assets find that what they have is not enough to meet their needs and expenditure. There is no way of knowing this simply by looking at what you have and comparing it to others. It may make you feel okay if you hear that, 'Actually, everyone else is similar to you,' but this doesn't mean you are in the same position whatsoever. This shows, in itself, that using external factors to satisfy your internal ease is problematic, because even if your mind is momentarily 'satisfied' by this, it might actually be a false sense of security.

You have to craft your own security internally, because this is where it comes from in the first place. From that point, more advantageous experiences can emerge.

Again, as with all of the previous chapters, the message is the same: the true nature of your experiences and a sense of well-being are manifested within your mind and then projected outwards onto the world, not the other way around. With this understanding, you can create some distance between your inner peace and external factors such as material objects, comparisons or other measures of 'success'. Uncoupling these gives you space to think and *be*. You can then approach your possessions, purchases and 'status' from a point of greater clarity. From there, you will be able to make more appropriate decisions as to why you may or may not acquire something.

Here's what good thinking around this looks like:

- 'Do I really need or want this or is it really for other people?'
- 'Am I compromising anything by getting this?'
- 'Will I still want it a week/month/year later?'
- 'Will it bring me peace of mind or security?' (Trick question!)
- 'Will I get enjoyment or positive experiences from this, even knowing that my well-being is still intact with or without this purchase?'

If you can answer these questions satisfactorily (and truly), then go ahead. The whole idea behind this book is not to live entirely free of materialism but to identify the true reasoning behind your decisions and no longer let money interact negatively with your peace of mind. You don't need to compare your external manifestations with those of others; your satisfaction is internal, as is theirs. We are all crafting our own realities and that is where the work begins.

I hope now that you can use your money in a way that truly aligns with your own values, rather than what you perceive to be the values of others.

22

Enjoy and Respect a Sudden Financial Windfall

"The sweetest honey
Is loathsome in his own deliciousness
And in the taste confounds the appetite.
Therefore love moderately; long love doth so;
Too swift arrives as tardy as too slow."

—*Friar Laurence, Shakespeare's* Romeo and Juliet

A FINANCIAL SITUATION THAT is becoming increasingly common in modern times is 'sudden wealth syndrome'. This is when someone with little financial experience or levels of wealth suddenly has a significant sum of money bestowed on them. While this holds true for lottery winners, the most obvious example is through a large inheritance or a swift business success. With the baby boomer generation owning the vast majority of wealth in most developed nations, this wealth is in the process of migrating to the next generation at a growing pace.

While this large transfer of wealth seemingly offers an increase in financial options for those receiving it, it can cause complications and needs to be addressed with balance and clarity, and at arm's length. You've probably heard the stories about lottery winners who went on a spending spree and used up all their prize money in a matter of months. While this is an extreme example, a significant windfall, if not approached properly, can have implications for the well-being of the recipient. These can manifest in various ways. Some people are overwhelmed by the sheer volume of options that they now have compared to what they had before because there is no gradual adjustment process. Of course, some then go on to spend their windfall on nonsense items because they've chased the immediate pleasure of consumption, so the money goes to waste. Again, this illustrates the destructive nature of desire and attachment that Buddhist principles argue against. Shakespeare covered this idea perfectly in the quote from Romeo and Juliet that introduces this chapter. The sweetness of indulgence can distort the taste itself. Pleasure, when pursued without moderation, can erode its own satisfaction. Alternatively, other people become so overwhelmed by the added responsibility that they do absolutely nothing with the money for the betterment of their financial lives.

Let's take Mr and Mrs H as an example. Their small business was offered a significant short-term contract with a public service that turned them into millionaires in a matter of months. They found that their attachment to money was increasing rapidly and that they were using a lot of their mental energy trying to work out what to do with all that money. They found that their levels of happiness and well-being actually *fell* when they had a significant amount of money flowing through their bank accounts. Their consumption radically increased but the enjoyment that they derived from their purchases diminished rapidly.

Mr and Mrs H also found that people started treating them differently and this was very difficult to come to terms with. They found it very uncomfortable and their overall well-being was affected even though the stress of financial security had been taken away. They found that other stresses arose to replace the stress of money and they were no better off internally. This helped them to realise that, while it was great to have plenty of money, their financial situation and their overall well-being were not in harmony. This is because the money was just that: money. Their thinking around the money created their negative experience. They are now living in this new-found position with the money very much in service to them, not the other way round.

One common response when people advocate that money doesn't buy happiness is that it's very easy to say this *when you have money.* This is a completely understandable position; but there is some wisdom to be gained from people who previously worried about money but then discovered that, once their financial concerns were alleviated, they were no happier as a result. It forces one to look inward and explore where the source of true well-being lies.

As we have learned – and will continue to learn –throughout this book, your well-being and experiences in life are very much manifested from the inside out, not the other way around. Mr and Mrs H found themselves less happy, all things considered, when money had lost all value to them. While we know that their well-being was intact all along, with or without money, their experience does highlight that more money does not necessarily mean more internal wellness. The moral of the story is that serenity cannot and will not come from the outside or material world. Why was material success debilitating for them? Because they were looking at money as the tool on which their happiness depended, when really it didn't hold that power: it was how they were *thinking* about the money that made things difficult. Now that they have discovered this for themselves, they are in a strong financial position which they treat with respect and distance, while focusing their minds on their internal wellness as a separate matter – the best of both worlds.

Not all of us will be so lucky as to receive a large financial injection through inheritance, a lottery win or a big business success; but the great lesson here is that we don't need this to be at peace internally. Having money is great and internal peace is great, but the two are not chained together. This is easier to see when you understand how the mind works and what all this ancient wisdom has been teaching us for thousands of years. It is just as relevant today as it was millennia ago, which really does tell you something: it's true.

When you realise that money is just an external and rather abstract concept, you can look at it with a bit less obsession and have greater choice over how you interact with it. A good approach if your financial position changes significantly could look like this:

- Work out what you want the money to do for you, not what you can do for the money – you are in control of your well-being, not the money. It is your servant, not your master.
- Invest it wisely to secure your future (remember that this is coming and will one day be your present), pay off bad debts, start a business, adjust your working patterns or take some time for yourself to adjust and figure things out – decide whatever it may be that you want your life to look like.

- Appraise your tax liabilities and how you may wish to manage them effectively.
- Get help if you don't have the time or inclination to do this yourself.
- Don't forget that all you have is the present moment, so spending some of the money is good, but you should do this knowing that you have got the basics right. After all, there will be other present moments that you might want to enjoy. You can then enjoy the experience that your money has brought you, rather than spending aimlessly (like the lottery winners who blew it all), thinking that this will give you comfort – it won't. Only you can do that from within because you create your experiences through thought in the moment.

Once you've figured out how to structure everything, without attachment and without emotional, thought-driven obsession and stress, you can move on with your life and enjoy a free mind and a freer financial position. You may even decide not to do anything for a while. That's fine too, as long as you've adopted a clear and calm approach and tuned in to what makes up your experiences around this new-found position. At least then, you'll know that the decision was a sound one.

Check in from time to time, reappraise your objectives, make adjustments where necessary and then go back to enjoying the moment! Thinking about the endless things that you can do with your money will only cause you to obsess and will let it control you again.

You are the one who calls the shots.

23

Take Control of Your Financial Life and Become its Master Again

"Action is the antidote to despair."

—*Joan Baez*

THIS QUOTE FROM singer, songwriter and activist Joan Baez is a powerful reminder that movement and decisiveness can dissipate the paralysing grip of fear, procrastination and overwhelm – forces that often govern financial decision-making. This wisdom highlights the necessity of taking action, even when faced with the emotional and cognitive barriers that arise when managing money. While this quote is from a more contemporary individual, it is grounded in ancient wisdom.

When people are trapped in the spiral of external tasks and challenges – whether due to fear of making the wrong decision or the inertia of avoidance – they often stagnate, leading to missed opportunities and compounding stress. Baez's quote underscores that action, however small, is the key to breaking this cycle. It shifts focus from rumination to resolution, helping to reclaim a sense of agency and clarity. You guessed it: the power comes back to you by impartially observing your thoughts and reshaping your experiences.

Another profound way in which you can become the master of your money is to stop dilly-dallying over financial decisions or actions. When you're in a reactive thought space or attempting to make financial decisions from an emotionally charged position, it can become debilitating. This leads to poor decisions, poor financial outcomes or no action whatsoever as you bury your head in the sand in an attempt to avoid the stress that you think it's causing you (when in fact you are creating this stress through your own thoughts). It is not the task at hand that has the power to cause you stress; you shouldn't give something so abstract a hold over you. It is your own generated experience that is making things stressful.

A financial decision is best made from a pragmatic, logical and rational perspective. Without this, your thoughts can turn to fear, greed, procrastination or ego. When decisions are made here, it is not your true self making them, but rather the mind trying to justify itself and please one of its many personas. Often, fear of a wrong decision can lead people to take no action at all. They don't always realise how much this is actually costing them in terms of lost opportunities. If they had to physically pay the price of those lost opportunities out of their bank accounts, it would likely be a very different story and they'd spring into action to stop such losses from arising. But when it's a hidden or opportunity cost, for some reason it is treated differently. A clear and pragmatic mind that understands the true nature of its experiences will be able to look at this a bit more objectively.

Take your tax affairs as an example. Many will follow the thought process that tax affairs are complicated and there is too much complex administration involved. This can manifest as thoughts of stress or hard work (e.g. dealing with the tax office), which can lead an individual to disregard the need to manage their tax affairs or reduce their tax bill – even if logically this is the best thing to do for their financial security. Many individuals, for example, know that moving money to higher-interest accounts or putting money in their pension or another tax-efficient vehicle will ultimately help them to bolster their finances, but thoughts of the stress or complication involved result in the dreaded dilly-dallying.

I have worked with many people like this during my career and could count at least 50 examples. One such example is Mr M, a client of mine who is a successful entrepreneur running a couple of businesses. Whenever we meet, I have some great ideas for him to make better use of the money that both he and his businesses are earning. Unfortunately, he struggles with administration in his personal life because he always prioritises his business operations. Ultimately, this often prevents him from taking advantageous actions because the thought of filling out another form fills him with dread (even though the form only takes around five minutes to complete and I do most of it for him). When I asked for a form to be filled out, a thought was generated about how much hassle that might be, a feeling of stress emerged and ultimately he put it off because there were other things going on, despite this simple action being far more financially beneficial for him than the entire prior week he had spent working. This is an extreme example of the opportunity cost of inaction. Clarity of mind and action would have avoided this outcome and the experience would not have been stressful at all. Again, this is proof that our manifestations, rather than the outside world, create our experiences. There is a well-known saying: 'You can lead a horse to water but you can't make it drink.' This is true, but a well-cultivated inner space would likely give the horse the right motivations to quench its thirst in the first place.

With an outside-in perspective (which is a false perspective), you think it's the task ahead that is affecting how you feel about it, so you avoid doing it to take that feeling away. When you realise it is your mind generating the thoughts from the inside out, you understand that you have some level of control over how you feel about the task at hand. It is just a task, and how stressful or difficult it may be is determined by how your mind decides to think about it.

With this understanding, you can simply action things when you need to action them, without a spiralling thought-led experience that makes them far more complicated than they need to be – and you'll ultimately be better off for it. You have probably already realised that thinking about doing a task is always more difficult than actually doing it. That is quite simply because your mind creates the feelings that you experience when responding to something; but once you actually get on with things, the reality is rather different. Why live like this? Why not feel easy before the task, during the task and after it?

24

Letting Go and Loosening the Grip

"Receive wealth or prosperity without arrogance; and be ready to let it go."

—*Marcus Aurelius*

ROMAN EMPEROR MARCUS Aurelius was a Stoic and one of the most significant figures of ancient times. His wisdom has been relevant for millennia and remains so today. If you haven't read his *Meditations* (private writings that probably weren't meant for publication but later became known), I strongly recommend that you do. They are a magnificent collection of his internal thoughts and spiritual clarity. He argues that true wisdom lies in recognising the impermanence of wealth and approaching it with humility and detachment. To receive wealth without arrogance means to understand that prosperity is not a reflection of one's inherent value but rather a transient circumstance. To be ready to let it go speaks to the Stoic principle of acknowledging that external possessions, no matter how abundant, do not define our inner peace or ultimate happiness. This also correlates with what we now understand about how our experiences are formed and how our minds work. Money is simply a tool to be used effectively for a purpose: it is nothing more than that. In addition, Buddhism teaches us that money itself is neither good nor evil; it is simply a resource. It only becomes problematic if we treat it with desire and/or attachment. This, Buddhists would argue, is where suffering comes from.

Some of us have more wealth, relative to our long-term needs, than we will ever need in many lifetimes. This is the case not just for the super-rich billionaires out there but for many 'normal' people too who have lived so frugally that they have amassed a lot of money but fail to utilise any of it for their own enjoyment or to make any changes to maximise its impact.

Mr and Mrs W – in their mid-80s and late 70s, respectively – are a perfect example of this. They live a comfortable life, with all their needs met by something as modest as the pension income they receive from the state. This is due to a lifetime of thrift and living below their means. While financial prudence is a positive sign of not having too much attachment to money and the material world, this can also go the other way and be taken too far. Mr and Mrs W now have over £1 million in accessible money and even more than that in property. They are getting older and health issues are starting to surface. They fully admit that they will never spend any of this money and are anxious about the significant inheritance tax that their estate will be liable for once it inevitably passes to their children.

When discussing what we could do to get around these potential issues, their responses were a perfect display of the outside-in approach to how the external world (in this case, money) impacts well-being:

- "I just like seeing it there."
- "If something bad happens, I can use it."
- "It makes me feel safe."
- "This is how we've always had it."
- "I know this makes no sense but I can't change it; it's a big jump."

These responses are clearly a sign of contradiction between rationality and logic and a thought-felt emotional response. Mr and Mrs W understand pragmatically that they could give some money to their children now, set up a trust, make charitable contributions, spend their money or invest it differently to manage their inheritance tax position; but their thinking about and outside-in attachment to the money in its current form are having long-term financial implications. A few simple changes could save hundreds of thousands of pounds; but instead of being driven by logic, they are driven by emotion and a misunderstanding of the relationship between money and their sense of internal security and well-being. Thankfully, once they understood this, Mr and Mrs W were able to strike a balance and the situation is now much better both for them and for future generations of their family. All this came from a simple realisation of where their thinking was around the issue. They simply changed their thinking and the reality changed. Everyone was happy with it.

Here are some questions that we can ask from this point of clarity (which can be applied to many financial decisions, not just this one):

- 'How much do we *really* need?'
- 'What do we want our life to look like at this stage?'
- 'Is there anything we've always wanted to do for ourselves that attachment to money has stopped us from doing?'
- 'Is our view on what constitutes "safety" logical or emotional?'
- 'What is in our best interests and the best interests of our loved ones on a long-term basis?'
- 'What are the potential disadvantages of making a big change? How could we mitigate them?'
- 'Can a balance be struck?'
- 'What are the potential disadvantages of taking no action whatsoever?'

Remember, your mind's natural state is one of peace and stillness. It is your thoughts and their manifestations that get in the way. If you sense that your thinking is more emotional than rational, you can try a different approach. For some, letting go is the most profitable outcome: you don't want irrational thoughts costing you money, even if at first it seems that this is not the case.

25

Achieving Monetary Harmony in Relationships

"Wealth is for the sake of life, not life for the sake of wealth."

—*Aristotle.*

THIS PIECE OF wisdom from Aristotle reminds us that money is a means to an end, not the end itself. It exists to support and enrich our lives; but when it becomes the central focus, it can strain even our closest relationships. In the context of a partnership, this perspective takes on added importance. If money becomes the dominant force in a relationship, it can distort priorities, create conflict and diminish the shared joy and purpose that bring two people together.

At the heart of financial disharmony in relationships lies the reality of our minds. Each of us has unique thoughts, beliefs and emotional attachments to money, shaped by our upbringing, experiences and personal narratives. These internal dynamics often manifest outwardly in how we approach shared finances

– whether through differing spending habits, saving priorities or attitudes towards risk.

Understanding the inside-out nature of our experiences can transform how we navigate financial disagreements. External conflict over money is rarely the real issue: it is often a reflection of internal insecurities, fears or desires projected onto our partner. By recognising this, couples can step back, reframe the situation and approach financial discussions with greater empathy and clarity.

Money is often a contentious issue in relationships. In fact, it is frequently touted as one of the biggest contributors to divorce in the Western world. Throughout my career, I have sat around the meeting table with hundreds of couples to discuss their financial planning. What comes up quite often is a disagreement within a marriage as to what the best course of action should be, as each views the same situation completely differently. Again, this is further evidence that the true nature of our experiences begins internally. Understanding this can help a couple to take a step back and understand that neither approach is right or wrong – just different. This fosters a greater respect for and understanding of the other person's position, which can eventually lead to reconciliation, compromise and a mutually agreeable path forward.

I have encountered many examples of this situation, but one that comes to mind is that of Mr and Mrs T. Mr T is very comfortable with taking risks: he speculates on the stock market and cryptocurrencies, has multiple business ventures and interests, and doesn't care at all if money is lost. To him, that's all part of the journey. Mrs T, however, has a much more cautious and conservative approach to their household finances: she likes to keep all her savings in bank accounts and pay off any debts with whatever else they have spare. When discussing a plan to bolster their retirement provisions and save for the future, we often reach a crossroads where the couple cannot agree on how to go about things. Mr T speaks with conviction and absolute certainty that his vision of taking higher investment risk and investing in new ventures is the correct one. Equally, Mrs T is totally convinced that this approach is reckless and that her safer approach is correct. Who is right here? The honest answer is neither – or both! As we have discovered, we all have a different version of reality based on our mind's projections. How liberating would it be, next time you're faced with a difference of opinion in your relationship (financial or otherwise), to draw on this understanding and have fun with it?

In this case, a compromise was found. Mr T kept a small pot of funds available to allow him to speculate on the markets without risking the couple's overall financial approach, which involved pursuing a more considered investment strategy for their future planning in order to manage the risks of leaving too much in the bank or spending too much on paying down debt. Mrs T was happy because some of their surplus income was being used to reduce their liabilities, meaning that these would be paid off by retirement. This couple are a rather extreme example but had either of them got their own way entirely, it would have been suboptimal for the achievement of their goals (one would occasionally have been taking uncalculated risks, while the other would have forgone the opportunity to make their money work for them over the long term). Instead, the compromise resulted in a situation where they were both satisfied and successfully struck a balance between risk, reward and safety.

Knowing that they had control over their thinking, and thus their experiences, Mr T was less attached to risky speculation and the potential for gains, while Mrs T felt more comfortable with some element of uncertainty in order to get more out of their financial situation in the long run.

As Aristotle's quote teaches us, money is ultimately the servant of our lives and not the purpose itself. By following this teaching, a couple can likely agree on how they want their money to serve them, rather than how they can serve their money. This can lead to compromise and a considered approach, balancing growth, accumulation and risk management while keeping the wider goal front and centre, rather than focusing on the journey needed to get there. We have already understood from ancient Chinese wisdom that balance is the key to a harmonious environment, and this is no different in the case of our relationships and the financial decisions that we make within them.

In this context, a discussion around money in a relationship can cause us to project from emotion rather than rationality. A healthier approach could involve answering some of the following questions:

- 'What are we trying to achieve here?'
- 'What is our ultimate goal?'
- 'How do we both want to get there?'
- 'Where do we disagree and where do we agree?'
- 'What compromises could be made?'
- 'Would a solution based on these compromises still achieve our goals and plans?'

- "Do I feel strongly about this particular course of action because it's rational and logical or because it creates an emotional response?"
- "Am I opposing this approach out of clarity and rationality or am I opposing it out of fear, desire or attachment?"

It's important to ask whether you are fuelled by desire or attachment in this process or whether you are thinking clearly from a still place. The latter, I assure you, will create a much more harmonious environment when planning your finances with your partner. It will also lead to better financial outcomes.

26

A Mindful Approach to Separation

> "Do not dwell in the past, do not dream of the future, concentrate the mind on the present moment."
>
> —*The Buddha*

THIS PROFOUND WISDOM from the Buddha is not just true of how to approach difficult times in our lives but also a great template for approaching life in general. There is a distinct difference between logical planning and decision-making borne out of worry or fear. The former allows for the effective utilisation of the mind's capabilities; whereas the latter is a misuse of the power that we all have at our disposal. Divorce or separation from a long-term partner is clearly a very difficult thing to go through and, for many, retaining the calmness and clarity of our natural state of being is extremely difficult in these circumstances. This is not an attempt to diminish the difficulty, but rather to allow for a more stable and rational approach to navigating it. An uncertain future, combined with the troubles and hurts of the past, can give rise to a very problematic experience – especially where money and children are concerned.

Divorce or separation involves disentangling shared lives, legal considerations, financial settlements, enormous amounts of administration and changes to living arrangements. It is an inherently arduous and overwhelming exercise. When you combine the uncertainty with the pain of separation and the past events that have led to it, it's easy to see how we can let the outside world completely inform our experiences and lead to emotionally charged decision-making. Yet it is during these troubled times that a clear and calm mind is most vital for better thinking and better experiences. The energy of the stimuli (i.e., the events in the outside world) may be stronger, but it is still absolutely true that it is your own mind interpreting those stimuli and projecting your experiences back out into the world. While it may be harder to remember this truth in difficult times, that's when the lesson becomes most important. It will create some space in your mind to approach the challenge in a clearer, more insightful way. The inside-out understanding of how our minds create our experiences can be an anchor during this turbulence.

Divorce often gives rise to strong feelings such as anger, betrayal, fear and regret. All of these are natural responses. However, by recognising in the moment when these feelings arise and understanding that they are generated by you, rather than imposed by the external world, you can regain some control. The past cannot be undone and the future is unknowable. By focusing on the present moment, free from judgements shaped by past pain or future fears, you can navigate this process more effectively. It may even mean that you surrender to the fact that you are currently unable to act effectively and should return to the process when you have regained more control. To incorporate the Buddhist view on 'attachment' again, particularly with divorce settlements, a bit of space between your well-being and financial issues will help you to determine what you need, why you need it and what is a fair compromise.

Divorce settlements can make it very difficult to control your responses to external stimuli and maintain your inner peace, for all the reasons above. Resentful and fearful decision-making can mean the situation takes a toll on you; jealousy can do likewise. There's a risk that the process could become less about the fair allocation of resources for all parties and more about resentment and one-upmanship – a situation for which the ego in pain is very much responsible. This is true for both sides in the negotiations. We all have our own realities and perceptions (because our minds interpret stimuli from the inside out), so each side has their own truth. It's important to recognise this to facilitate a healthier, more respectful approach for the benefit of everyone involved – particularly where children are concerned.

By understanding the inside-out nature of the mind and the wisdom that we have explored on the importance of the present moment, free of past and future, we can cultivate a more mutually respectful environment. From this point of clarity and compassion, decisions can be made that ensure mutual financial security and a better emotional environment both for any children and for each other.

Here are some helpful and respectful approaches that can be adopted when negotiating a financial settlement during a divorce:

- Have an early discussion on expectations and what each party needs.

- Make an early appraisal of how to sustain the financial security of your children.
- Remain on each task at hand without judgement; if you notice the emotive mind or ego stepping in to guide discussions, leave it and return only when you know that you are operating from a clear and rational space.
- Discuss what works harmoniously for everyone, especially where children are involved.
- Understand that there are different realities at play and yours is just one of them.
- Understand that the nature of how your mind interprets your experiences can create some distance between your true self and your noisy mind.
- Get help early via mediation if the other party is unable to approach the situation calmly; fighting back with more emotionally driven responses will only add fuel to the fire and create a negative feedback loop.
- Work together on how both of your goals and financial needs can be met and help each other to get there.

Approaching divorce in a mindful, peaceful way can help the process to become a bit lighter, freeing up your mind to focus on new insights and decision-making for your futures, rather than getting lost in the emotional turmoil of a separation. The difficulty is unavoidable, but the stress that you put yourself through (remember: it's you doing it to yourself, not the outside world doing it to you) will not make it any easier to get to where you need to be. A freer sense of emotional and monetary attachment will. It will also create some mental space to glean new insights into how to make the most of the opportunities and challenges that your new life promises via growth and renewal.

As we learned in the previous chapter, money is recognised as a key wedge in long-term relationships. It is often cited as a major contributor to divorce. While this chapter explores a more mindful approach to dealing with divorce and its financial implications, the adoption of a more emotionally detached approach to our finances earlier in our relationships could actually contribute to more stable relationships in general. With a deeper understanding of our experiences and how our minds form attachments and desires, we could indeed achieve greater harmony and compassion in our marital discussions on money and avoid the difficulty of divorce entirely. Of course, there will be times when divorce is absolutely the right course of action; but a clearer and wiser approach to your thinking around your relationships will ensure that the choices you make are the right ones, rather than being born out of unhelpful thinking.

27

A More Peaceful Journey in Your Career

"The pursuit, even of the best things, ought to be calm and tranquil."
—*Cicero*

Roman statesman and philosopher Cicero was well known for his wisdom. While he wasn't a Stoic himself, he urged the elite of Rome to adopt Stoic principles as a means of leading the city in a virtuous way. Cicero is often credited with influencing the modern laws that still operate in our society today. His teaching here is relevant to this chapter, which explores the career choices that we make and how money can affect them.

It is completely true that money is an important factor when making career choices. Of course, the numbers need to add up and you want to be suitably compensated for the work you do and the time you sacrifice to do it. However, it is also true that we often make decisions in our careers that are *purely* about the money, when most of the time the position is in fact much more nuanced.

When we attach too much of our sense of fulfilment, worth and well-being to the figure on our pay cheque, we are once again aligning our sense of internal ease with an arbitrary figure, and this may not be the right choice when considering other aspects of our lives. As Cicero states, the journey should be a calm and peaceful one. Do not make the mistake of viewing challenge and tranquillity as two opposing forces: they can work together harmoniously. In fact, challenging but rewarding work can be very satisfying. This isn't to say that job opportunities with higher pay cheques should simply be turned down because the work is harder; rather, that new opportunities should be assessed based on a multitude of factors, and not just money.

Time and again I have worked with clients who moved from jobs they loved to jobs they hated for extra money that they didn't need, to buy things that they didn't need. It always originates from thought, as conditioned patterns of thinking about money fuel external attachments and inform subsequent decision-making – another great example of the power of thought and how it can shape our life experiences. This hardly seems like a calm and tranquil way to approach career progression with the optimal goal of life satisfaction.

Mr F is a prime example. He had been browsing the job market and knew that his employer, which he loved working for, was paying him roughly 10% less than the market average for a similar role. The company wasn't flush with cash and after a pay negotiation, Mr F could only secure himself another 3–4% salary raise. His current role allowed him to work from home most of the week and was local to him. He also enjoyed the company culture and had a great relationship with his colleagues. Despite all this, he felt that a higher salary would be great: "Things might just feel a little easier." After exploring the other jobs available, he knew he would have to:

- travel two days a week;
- accept higher targets and an increased workload;
- spend less time with his family;
- work with a product that he was less passionate about; and
- work in a more 'cut-throat' company culture.

Mr F had attached his sense of internal ease to his finances and was really saying, 'It might make me feel more okay' to have a higher salary coming in every month. Luckily, after working through his savings plan, long-term objectives and family budget, it became clear that his financial goals could be achieved under his current structure and he decided not to change jobs. This is an example of reason leading the way, but I assure you that this is very often not the case! Sometimes the extra money, within a balanced and considered appraisal, may tip the scales; but adopting this approach should at least help you to feel comfortable that you have made the right decision.

Had Mr F enjoyed travel and been looking for a more challenging environment *and* more money, the correct decision might have been a different one. The key is that he regained control over his attachments and thoughts around his own security and made the best decision for him based on his values.

As we've already discovered on this journey, money is a tool, not the goal itself. How we use this tool is up to us; but when it becomes the goal, there is no way ever to achieve it and the outside world of money becomes your master once again.

To be clear, career progression can be a very rewarding and fulfilling endeavour; but money should be seen as a by-product of loving your work, finding your passion, doing a good job and enjoying something that doesn't feel like work. We've all heard the phrase, 'Love what you do and you'll never work a day in your life.' The reason we've all heard this so many times is because it is most likely true. As we've learned from Buddhist teachings, money is neither good nor bad; it is our attachment to it that causes suffering. We know from our understanding of the mind that our need for a higher pay cheque for the sake of it is usually born out of an emotional, thought-led response to the power of money. Ancient wisdom tells us that we can be happy with few material goods in our lives.

So, what does this mean? It means that career decisions or the jobs that we do should involve a clearer, more rational approach to how we think about money. Your ego might want a higher pay cheque, but what would you be sacrificing to earn it?

When considering a career move or a new job offer with a larger pay cheque, a clear, rational and logical mind would consider the following questions:

- 'Am I interested in the new role or am I ultimately doing it for the higher pay?'
- 'Do I believe in the culture and mission of the new company/ employer?'
- 'Am I likely to have the same job satisfaction as I currently enjoy?'
- 'How will it affect my family?'
- 'Do I want to change careers at some point and would now be a good time to do so?'

Only after weighing up these nuances should money play a role in your decision. It is far from the sole consideration. Money is just one *factor.*

Often, the pursuit of a higher pay cheque is driven not by genuine need but by thought patterns tied to fear, ego or societal expectations. Recognising these influences can help you to make clearer, more aligned decisions.

With a balanced approach to considering these factors, a career trajectory can be both lucrative and enjoyable. Both outcomes are possible simultaneously when genuine reasoning and purpose are driving your decisions.

28

Relieve the Financial Pressures of Early Family Life

"Do not spoil what you have by desiring what you have not; remember that what you now have was once among the things you only hoped for."

—*Epicurus*

ANCIENT GREEK PHILOSOPHER Epicurus was the founder of a school of philosophy known as Epicureanism, which shares some ideas with Stoicism, its contemporary. Both considered a good life to be tranquil, calm and without attachment. They differed in many ways too; but one consistency between the two schools of thought is their emphasis on gratitude, a peaceful existence and the pursuit of wisdom and self-inquiry.

The above pearl of wisdom from Epicurus leads us to what can often be a very challenging endeavour financially: raising children. As the father of two young children myself, I understand the significant costs, time constraints and personal sacrifice that come with nurturing and raising a child. It is also worth noting that I am not some guru when it comes to juggling work, finances, presence and parenthood. I have fallen foul of thought-fuelled experiences and projections many times over. You will also find that this still happens to you even after reading this book. The beauty of this learning, however, is that you can catch and identify such thinking a bit earlier in the thought cycle and recalibrate yourself to a more grounded position. This will allow a different experience to be born into reality. I will, of course, be focusing on the financial elements in this chapter, but the same underlying philosophy can be applied to the general stresses that inevitably arise when raising a family.

Clothes, school costs, food, childcare bills, bigger cars, extra bedrooms, trips, entertainment, books, toys, presents – they all add up to what, for the vast majority of families, are eyewatering costs. In this situation, it's easy to revert to the outside-in approach to mind: 'This is so expensive and it's causing me/us a lot of stress and personal suffering.' While it's easy to understand how this can happen, it's important to remember during these times that raising young children is among the greatest and most virtuous things that a person can do in their life. It involves enormous effort but comes with such wondrous rewards. If you have had young children who have now flown the nest, you'll likely tell people with a young family: 'Make the most of it – it goes by so quickly.' Those with young children will be all too familiar with this advice from the older generation. But the reason this common wisdom prevails is because it's true.

When you understand that your experiences are manifested internally and then projected out onto the world, you discover that you have a choice as to how you experience hardship. You can choose to be stressed over the financial constraints of raising a family or you can choose to be present in the moment and realise that you are probably experiencing some of the best years of your life. The financial implications of having a family will not be going away for a while: either you can enjoy the ride in a tranquil, loving and peaceful way or you can lose these years to your mind's incredible ability to tell you that things aren't okay. The conscious state, by its very nature, is still and peaceful. The mind's job is to problem solve – and it is very good at that. It is, however, crucial to look at the mind objectively and learn how to use it as a tool when it is really needed. There is a part of you that is able to observe and watch your thoughts (otherwise, you wouldn't know you're thinking!), and this place of stillness affords greater clarity when interpreting the stimuli you receive.

The societal pressures that come with children are impossible to ignore: where you went at the weekend, what your kids are wearing, the games they play and the holidays they go on. Attaching your well-being to such pressures causes no end of suffering and inner disturbance. At the end of the day, our children want to feel loved, listened to, nurtured and supported. In so doing, you are approaching family life with stillness and presence. If you have a tight budget due to significant fixed costs, remember that your well-being and that of your children is not derived from the material world: you don't need to be influenced by what others are doing in order to give your children a nurturing home. Some of the best days that you can have with your children are spent out in nature or, indeed, in your own living room – neither of which costs anything. The wisdom of Epicurus is profound in that you don't want to spend the most experientially rich part of your life craving more money or a better budget only to wish, later on in life, that you'd been more present at the time.

Children naturally live in the present moment: they don't dwell on past mistakes or worry about future challenges. By spending time with them and engaging in their world, we have an opportunity to reconnect with this innate ability to be present. We know that this mental clarity is possible because children are a great reflection of it and we were all children once. It takes adults a bit of inner work to unravel a conditioned and habitual mindset, but it *is* possible.

Here is some practical guidance on how to manage the financial strains during this critical life phase:

- Sit down once a month and draw up your family budget for the month based on fixed expenditure set against household income (always allowing for an emergency/contingency aspect).
- Look back over the previous month and assess it against your previous budget.
- Discuss openly where the strengths and weaknesses in the family budget are and what you can and can't realistically afford.
- Prioritise the most meaningful, nurturing and developmentally rich activities for your family.
- Remind yourself that your inner clarity and sense of wellness are not derived from the external, material world and plan from a point of clarity and reason. If you find yourself in an emotionally reactive space, return when you're in a more tranquil frame of mind.

- Allow for regular savings and a long-term plan if the budget allows.

Once you have done this exercise, you can move on, knowing where you stand financially. This allows you and your children to be fully present and engaged in the moment: your love, attention and thoughts will be firmly on them rather than the money-mind attachment. The simplest way to ease the financial pressure on family life is not to let it burden you, no matter how tight your budget may feel. You can do this with less attachment. You could find that there may also be some space for refinement and further savings which could bolster your financial resources.

29

Invest with Purpose and Clarity

"Endurance is one of the most difficult disciplines, but it is to the one who endures that the final victory comes."

—*The Buddha*

SOME OF MY favourite lessons in patience, endurance and tranquillity come from Buddhist principles. This quote from the Buddha provides a perfect introduction to what can be a difficult concept for some to grasp: investing your money. Whether in property, the stock market, our own businesses or ourselves through education, investing money can be an incredibly rewarding endeavour, both financially and personally.

However, there are a number of things that stop us from investing, such as budget constraints, risk aversion, discomfort with uncertainty and, ultimately, an emotional attachment to money that is neither healthy nor rational. Where budget constraints are concerned, I truly hope that reading this book has helped you to detach slightly from the illusion that the material world informs your well-being. A natural by-product of this could be the refining of a lower budget or expenditure, thus freeing up spare funds to invest for your future. If you are risk averse, we have already discovered that there are calculated risks and reckless risks: the former result rationally from our still and clear minds, while the latter usually derive from emotionally charged greed and an ego-influenced perspective. The clear and rational approach fundamentally understands risk and is comfortable with it. This is because it affords a bit of space between a person's well-being and the temporary valuations of their investments (or short-term costs incurred to date).

A freer space between you and your money should make you less reckless and less risk averse, and should hopefully allow you to approach your long-term financial planning in a more balanced and nuanced way. Investing money in your future situation, as already discussed, can be hugely rewarding in the long run. Compounded growth on investments and sensible financial assets has done a great job of providing financial (but not mental!) security for participants since the dawn of capitalism. It helps to protect wealth against the erosive power of inflation over time, affords financial options and breathing room at times of uncertainty, and enables people to align their money with the general productivity and innovation of mankind over the long term.

Naturally, many of us are investors without giving this much consideration. We have wealth tied up in our homes (the property market) and our pension funds (the stock markets and other financial markets); and we invest in our education to develop our power to earn in jobs that we find fulfilling and interesting. The rewards of doing so are clear. Therefore, I ask you: why is it that we don't fret too much over the value of our homes compared with other financial assets that we can see daily on a screen? The answer again is the money-mind attachment. It has become easier than ever to invest and track the fluctuations in the value of our money on a day-by-day, minute-by-minute basis. As a result, if we fail to counteract our outside-in conditioning, we will fail to access our consciousness and stillness, which can lead to erratic behaviour (e.g., reckless greed or risk aversion).

A clear and free mind is open to assessing different investment options and understands the pros and cons, tax implications, risks and rewards, as well as the potential consequences of *not* doing anything. From this clearer standpoint, you can make informed investment decisions, knowing that you have done so from a considered position, and then move on with your life and enjoy the present moment once again.

The world of investing is inherently volatile and uncertain: that is the price you pay for the reward you get in the long term. As the quote from the Buddha at the start of this chapter clearly states, enduring this uncertainty is what yields the benefits in the long run. The key to undertaking the journey in a calm and tranquil way is to understand the true nature of how your experiences are formed and lean into the wisdom that we have explored together in this book. We have control over how we interact with our thoughts around money and our subsequent experiences with it.

There are, of course, both sensible ways and more speculative ways of approaching this. I suggest that you get clued up on the financial markets by reading books on investing and diversifying sensibly. For many, the answer is to seek professional assistance to guide you through the journey and help you make decisions. My objective with this book, as previously explained, is not to teach you how to invest, how to get rich or what to buy/invest in with your money. My objective is to try to help you separate well-being from money, so that you can do the necessary work yourself from a more reasoned and logical position. There are hundreds, if not thousands, of books out there that can help you with the next phase by offering practical tips on financial planning. A qualified financial planner can also help with this if you really do want to detach from money and focus on other parts of your life!

Some healthy and logical questions to start asking yourself could include the following:

- 'Do I have enough of a safety net for emergencies before I consider investing any money?'
- 'If my investments suffered for a while, how would this impact my life, if at all?'
- 'What do I want to achieve in the long run? What would my life look like in the future if I could choose an outcome?' (Think about how you live your life here, not how much money you want.)
- 'What do I need to put away to afford that lifestyle?'
- 'How much risk is sensible considering my timelines and personal circumstances?'
- 'What are the risks of continuing as I am? Is there a shortfall? Can I fund my future life with my current savings plan or current expenditure?'
- 'Do I need this money any time soon?'
- 'What expenditure can I review in order to create space for an emergency fund or future investments to avoid living month to month, pay cheque to pay cheque?'

- 'Has my previous attitude to saving or investing been driven by my calm, conscious and rational mind or by an emotional attachment or experience?'

With these types of questions cleared up, and after a period of monetary introspection, you can remove some of the previous hindrances to your future rewards and approach investing from a more realistic and logical perspective.

30

Allocating Your Money and Moving On

"Patience is bitter, but its fruit is sweet."

—Aristotle

HERE IS ANOTHER key piece of ancient wisdom from Aristotle – a simple yet profound truth, telling us that while it is often difficult to be patient, the results can be profound over time. This is also applicable to our relationship with money, our tendency to have a reactionary relationship with our thoughts and indeed the premise of this chapter: that locking money away can be very advantageous if we do it right.

One pain point – particularly with young people – when I approach the subject of saving for retirement or a long-term future goal is the length of the process at hand. Many of the challenges that I face here stem from the role of pensions in retirement planning. Of course, in most economically advanced countries, pensions offer very attractive tax relief for anyone saving through them – with the caveat that, once you put money in, you can't get it out until you are older. This delayed access is a sticking point for many people, as they want to know that they can access their money if they need it, despite the overwhelming incentives not to do so. Again, this challenge is usually an emotional rather than a rational one, in that your well-being and peace are once again being tied together incorrectly, thus preventing you from organising your finances optimally for the future you (who will invariably exist at some point!). Patience, as Aristotle clearly outlines, can produce significant rewards. This same principle is true in general for your relationship with money in uncertain times; and it's just as true when looking at how you allocate the resources that you have available.

If you need easy access to every penny you own just to feel okay, then you will only be okay if that is the case. If you can learn that you are okay anyway by spending some time observing these thoughts, you can start using the tools at your disposal more effectively.

Have you ever avoided an optimal financial decision, tax-planning exercise or financial opportunity simply because you simply like 'seeing it [your money] there' or being able to 'access it if the world falls apart'?

There are, of course, perfectly good reasons why you might not tie up all your money for long periods of time or overinvest so that you have no contingency plan. But there are also times when the decision to avoid allocating funds effectively is born out of attachment and the desire to feel okay because you think that your sense of security is underpinned by having access to money. Only when you separate mind and money and incorporate some rational wisdom can you tell what the right course of action is.

Consider the example of Mr and Mrs B, clients I have worked with for a number of years. They both earn a high wage and their income exceeds their required expenditure. They have a solid emergency fund that would keep them covered in the event of a job loss for at least six months. They also have some investments that have provided them with good, compounded growth over the years. By all accounts, they are doing quite well in the financial sphere. However, when I first met with them and brought up the topic of retirement provisions and long-term goals, I discovered that they had both opted out of their workplace retirement savings schemes, which would have given them significant tax relief to the tune of 45% for one and 40% for the other. In addition, their employer offered to pay 10% of their salary as long as they contributed 10% of their own salary into their pensions. The 10% 'free' contributions from their employer plus the significant tax savings on these vehicles represented extremely attractive savings incentives for them both. When I queried why they had forgone such significant benefits, for which their future selves would be very thankful, it all boiled down to the fact that they would rather have 55–60% pay after tax than the full amount in their pensions plus another full amount paid in by their employer. The root cause of this choice was that if anything went wrong, it would be a long time before they could access the money. They felt this way even though they had other accessible money for such eventualities, and more than enough disposable income for the life that they were currently leading.

Can you see what happened in this situation? Mr and Mrs B's sense of comfort was aligned with the nominal figure on their pay cheques rather than the real nature of their experiences – from the inside out. Attachment and desire had won the day: the couple were paying more tax on money that they did not need because of a mind-money connection that wasn't really true. Luckily, they both recognised the issue (by changing their thinking) and have now re-enrolled in the scheme, putting themselves on track for a sustainable financial future while still having a balanced and meaningful life in the present. They not only are continuing to live the same life they had before but also have a vehicle which is invested for the long term, providing growth plus tax relief and employer contributions that compound the effect.

Understanding this wisdom and the true reasons for the financial decisions you make allows you to take a more balanced approach to long and short-term goals, letting the power of patience do a lot of the hard work for you. Such detachment also allows you to do so in an easier, more peaceful way.

Some insightful questions that you can ask yourself when balancing long and short-term goals include the following:

- 'What is holding me back? Is it my busy thoughts or emotional attachment, or is there a logical and fundamental explanation?'
- 'What is my fallback plan if I lose access to some of these funds and something happens in my life?'
- 'Do I really need any more gratification from consumption or, on balance, does my future self need a bit extra?'
- 'How much do I need to save to continue my current lifestyle later in life when my earning capacity has diminished?'

- 'What are the advantages of forgoing access versus the disadvantages?
- 'Is my current standard of living improved by not putting money away or will it effectively stay the same?'
- 'Could I reach a point at a different stage in life when I might wish that I had saved more?'

Having appraised these questions, you can start to develop a sensible, logical plan to ensure that your current and future needs are met, rather than holding on to a misconceived idea that your immediate access to money and sense of security are one and the same.

31

The Joy Derived from Gifting

"For where your treasure is, there your heart will be also."

—*Matthew 6:21*

IT WOULD BE remiss of me not to offer some wisdom from the Bible: after all, it is one of the most historically significant books that the world has ever seen. This quote from the Gospel of Matthew aligns with the argument that money itself is merely a tool, an energy. You can utilise this energy in a multitude of ways, but one particularly meaningful use for your money is to give some of it away. This could take many forms: helping out a family member, gifting to your children while you are still alive (I've heard this called 'gifting with warm hands'), making charitable donations or helping those in need. Great spiritual satisfaction and inner peace can be derived from gifting; but only a clear mind, free of the money-mind attachment, can make this possible. A clear mind can appraise your current financial situation, be at peace with monetary sacrifice and assess what you may have available to use for the benefit of others. As Matthew reminds us, how you use your monetary energy is where you find your heart. You can also substitute 'heart' for 'meaning', 'purpose' or 'love'. A relationship with money where it acts as a servant to your values, rather than being a master over you, is where true meaning can be found – both in your life and in the lives of others.

This isn't just a teaching from the Bible – it's a consistent and undeniable theme underpinning many of the great religions and ancient philosophies. Buddhists talk of *dana* (generosity), which involves sacrificing ownership of something for another, without expecting the favour to be returned. Stoic philosophers such as Seneca often discussed the role of generosity in living a virtuous life. Hindus believe in *karma*: the idea that your actions and choices in this life shape your future lives. This list is by no means exhaustive, but across cultures, the relationship between meaning and giving is a common currency.

When you become too attached to money and its power, you deprive yourself of the ability to use your available energy to benefit others. This does not mean that you should give all your money away or anything even remotely that drastic, as you still need money to sustain your own life and build for your future. However, by adopting the principles that we have discussed and gaining a freer relationship with money, you may just find some extra space to help others who are less fortunate than you.

There are, of course, times when giving can go too far. In my work, I've met people who have a poor relationship with money and feel so overwhelmed by its power that they choose to give away more than they are able to or should (usually through thought-driven avoidance, guilt or fear). I've also met people who have significant resources at their disposal and could never possibly spend all their money in their lifetimes but give little or nothing away. The art, of course, is in the balance.

Some insightful questions that you could ask yourself when contemplating giving include the following:

- ‘What causes or people bring me joy when I support them?’
- ‘How much money do I realistically need and what can I give away, gladly and safely?’
- ‘What legacy do I want to leave through my acts of generosity?’
- ‘Does my giving align with my values and goals, or am I giving out of obligation, guilt or insecurity?’

To many, giving money away feels like losing something valuable – a reduction of resources, a subtraction from security. This perception stems from the deep attachment that many of us have to money, viewing it not just as a tool but as an essential part of our identity and well-being. It is the mind’s work of bringing insecurity to life through thought.

When we understand that our experiences in the world are formed from the inside out and adopt more rational wisdom in our decision-making, the act of giving becomes far less about loss and far more about fulfilment.

32

Maintaining Family Harmony During Difficult Times

"Holding on to anger is like grasping a hot coal with the intent of throwing it at someone else; you are the one getting burned."

—*The Buddha*

One thing that I see in my work far too often for my liking is a deeply troubling family dynamic during difficult times, such as sickness or the loss of a family member. Disagreements between executors, attorneys and family members have broken many a family apart. The above quote from the Buddha explains this situation perfectly. Anger and frustration are very common in difficult situations, especially where money is concerned; but holding on to that anger can have long-term consequences for family unity which are not helpful, financially or otherwise. This again comes down to the mind's interpretation of an event or financial decision, leading to suboptimal responses. Finding that inner calm and wisdom before interacting with these difficult situations can make a dramatic difference in reconciling alternative viewpoints within families.

I have seen families break up over care options for a sick relative. I have seen families fall apart over disagreements on what to do with the money of a parent who has lost capacity. I have seen families take each other to court over the contents of a relative's will, never to speak again. I have seen children of wealthy parents try to get hold of their money too aggressively, causing the parents to back off and put up metaphorical walls around their financial affairs.

This often leads to financial paralysis where decisions are simply not made – or, at the very least, are not optimal for all involved – because the mind's attachment to how previous experiences made them feel is informing their thinking in the present moment. The attachment, of course, is each person seeking to get the outcome they want, to make themselves feel okay. If they simply understood that they could be okay anyway and approached the situation with greater mutual respect, rationality and clarity, perhaps a happy compromise could be reached. Understanding the true nature of your experiences and the blurred lines between 'hard reality' and personal preferences goes a long way towards facilitating mutual understanding and compromise.

As a good example of this, one long-term client lost capacity and developed dementia a few years ago. I had worked with the family for many years. Upon diagnosis and diminished capacity, I needed to bring the children (who had power of attorney) into the financial planning for this client, as he was no longer capable of understanding or making decisions on his own. There were evidently tensions between the three children and differences of opinion on what should be done about his money. They would individually write to me asking for completely different actions in relation to their father's money without consulting the others. Their relationship broke down fully and they started seeking legal advice against each other – completely forgetting that they were paying for an adviser, neutral of any internal family disputes, to advise them. They were so caught up in getting their own way against each other that their father's financial outcomes were hindered and my mission to do the best thing by their father was impossible to fulfil. This is the only time in my career thus far that I have had to walk away from a long-term professional relationship, and it saddened me deeply that the person suffering the most was an unwell man who had no idea what was going on.

This is an extreme but pertinent example of how our individual and internally manifested realities can be misconstrued as absolute truths. The thought/feeling-generated experience in this moment became so intense that the whole thing fell apart.

Had these siblings paused to look inward first and considered their own internal biases, they could have acted with clarity and compassion. Their father's well-being could have remained central, guiding decisions rather than becoming a casualty of their internal conflict.

As the quote at the start of this chapter implies, they all lost as a result of their anger. Had they acted from that still place which is accessible to us all, a compromise could have been reached: they could have agreed to listen to the guidance of a neutral adviser; or they could have approached each other from a position of mutual understanding that they each had their own versions of 'the truth' and a balance could have been struck.

Families have a lot of history – some good and some not so good. This is universal across most families the world over. As we have learned, our minds receive stimuli from the outside world and try to make sense of what is happening based on a long litany of previous experiences. In families, these past experiences run deep for all involved, going back as far as childhood. It is unsurprising that in difficult times and when money is concerned, responses become amplified. In this situation, it is crucial to access that part of your being that can look at your mind without judgement before interacting with the situation that you are facing. Otherwise, everybody suffers.

Healthy approaches in difficult times could include the following:

- Pay attention to your mind when communicating with family members on money matters. If it is disturbed, remember that feelings are impermanent and let them run their course before taking action. Never act out of pure emotion; find that inner peace first.
- Don't respond straight away. Observe your thoughts for a little while and understand where they are coming from.
- Acknowledge the position of the other with empathy and understanding and respectfully explain your own position.
- If you find that anger/resentment/frustration is coming back at you, suggest discussing this another time.
- Remind yourself that there is rarely one universal truth; there are multiple realities at play here.
- Be prepared to compromise.

By looking inward and paying attention to how our experiences are manifesting in the moment, we can take a step back, observe ourselves and tackle the decisions ahead with a deeper sense of compassion and effectiveness.

33

A Quieter Approach to Everything

"Be still. The quieter you become, the more you are able to hear."
— *Rumi and Ram Dass*

EVERYTHING THAT WE have explored so far with respect to our well-being and financial decision-making points to the undeniable benefits of creating a stiller, more peaceful inner space. The above quote from Rumi – a celebrated Persian poet – encapsulates the message that we have been exploring together. With stillness, greater awareness and helpful thinking can emerge. While the benefits extend far beyond the financial sphere, they can significantly improve this area of our lives, as well as everything else.

We have examined some key common areas of our monetary lives throughout this book. To go through every single financial decision is unnecessary, as you'll likely have got the point by now and I have repeated myself enough.

However, what we have worked through here applies to any financial situation that we find ourselves in. Consider the following examples:

- **The startup founder or self-employed businessperson expending their energy on worrying about how they could be busier:** This is neither profitable nor helpful. Noticing these thought patterns in real time can help still the mind and allow for more contemplation of what can be done to increase productivity.
- **The couple with young children who are so attached to the money flow that they cannot bring themselves to buy life insurance with 1% of their pay:** Letting go of these attachments and false ideals of external comforts will enable protection to be put in place, mitigating financial risk at a crucial time in life.
- **The recently retired person struggling to find purpose and identity in life after work:** An impartial observation may reveal that this identity is self-prescribed and new thinking could emerge that allows for a new purpose after a long career has ended.
- **The person scared of retiring despite being able to do so because they don't know who they are without their work:** A fresher, more open inner space can help to craft a vision for the next stage of life that is equally fulfilling and purposeful.
- **The person in hardship crushing themselves over lack of resources:** Letting go of deprecating thought mechanisms affords room for more growth-orientated thinking.
- **The person whose roof blows off in a storm and who must incur a major expense to rectify it:** Sitting with the negative

thoughts of parting with money and observing these thoughts without attachment will allow them to pass. This may create greater room internally for new thinking that finds a way to replace the funds spent on the roof.

- **The person who is stressed over sorting out their tax affairs and is rushing to get them finished:** Taking a step back and waiting for peace to arrive may dissipate the stressful thoughts; and you could remember an expense or tax relief that you forgot you could claim.

The list goes on and on – and the strategy applies to everything that we face out there in the world. Our thoughts play a crucial role in our outcomes and understanding this will enable us to develop a better relationship with money by investing some efforts in our internal space.

On that note, let's look at some wider perspectives to finish our journey together (and start yours).

Part Three

Some Final Perspectives

34

How to Be Wealthy Beyond Belief, Today

"He is richest who is content with the least, for content is the wealth of nature."

—*Socrates*

A BOOK LEANING INTO ancient wisdom from the great minds of the ages would not be complete without input from Socrates. As a reader, you may well be familiar with this ancient Greek thinker, often credited as the father of Western philosophy, who likely influenced the movement known as Stoicism. A key principle that Socrates taught is that, as a species, we are not upset by external events, but rather by our own judgements. This, of course, is another way of saying that our thoughts and feelings give rise to our experiences.

This leads into what we have been learning throughout this journey together about the reality of how our minds construct our experiences. To be wealthy is not simply to accumulate assets:

it means being content both in the journey and with what you have already. This is not to say that there is anything inherently wrong with accumulating wealth; but by being constantly dissatisfied with your financial situation, you are robbing yourself of true wealth, which is contentment. You can set financial goals, accumulate assets, grow your money and be content. You can also be content even if your financial situation is not where you wish it to be. The principle of contentment is not attached to wealth – they are two different things. One is internal (peace); the other is external (money). You can have both of these, one of them or neither. My entire argument throughout this book aims to help you reach one (peace), so that you have more mental freedom to work more optimally on the other (money).

If you feel yourself falling back into the money-mind cycle, try changing your reference point. The very fact that you have enough money to buy this book makes you one of the richest people in the world. The fact that you have exposure to money in some form means that you are rather well-off. The fact that you are living in the twenty-first century with a high average life expectancy, modern medicine, technology, transport and clean water, makes you very 'wealthy' indeed. You know this intrinsically, but the desire and attachment that lead us to compare our situation to those of others can cause us to lack contentment and inner peace.

By being content (while still having goals and aspirations), you are most of the way there – and certainly in a better mental space to make your financial goals more achievable and enjoyable.

35

The Certainty of Death and Embracing the Journey

"It is not death that a man should fear, but he should fear never beginning to live."

—*Marcus Aurelius*

MARCUS AURELIUS, WHOM we heard from earlier in the book, makes a powerful observation here about the fact of our own mortality. We start life with nothing and end it with nothing. Humans have been on this Earth for less than a microsecond of the planet's 4.5 billion-year existence. You are only here for a microsecond compared to the duration of humanity, let alone the history of the planet. The probability of you being here, at this time, in your current form, is so very improbable that it is as close to impossible as you could imagine.

By allowing the external world to manipulate our experiences and inner peace (financial or otherwise), we are giving up valuable time – time which we have very little of to begin with.

This, of course, is a much deeper and bigger discussion that goes far beyond the remit of this book; but it does serve as a profound reminder that the gift we have been given – the gift of being able to experience this world – is a short-lived one. The very fact that life is finite allows us to free ourselves up on the journey and make the most of it. A healthy relationship with money enables you to use it as a tool to align with your values, goals and objectives. Seeing money in this way will help you to live a fruitful, meaningful life both now and in the future. Money is not the goal itself. We are not here for very long and money is only one part of a life well lived.

Making sound financial decisions and providing security and resources for your family, business or retirement are important processes, which should be addressed with respect and rationality. However, you can do this freely and without obsession or attachment. Check in with your financial planning from time to time, make tweaks where necessary and then leave it alone. The world is out there to be enjoyed – freedom and clarity of mind will help you do just that.

36

Embracing Change and Uncertainty

"The only constant in life is change."

—Heraclitus

HERACLITUS WAS ANOTHER ancient Greek philosopher known for his deep self-inquiry, who pondered our connection to the universe even before Socrates. His well-known quote above is just as relevant today as it was more than 2,500 years ago. We all understand that change is inevitable – pick any period in the history of humanity and you will see the constant and unrelenting force of change weaving its way through the development of mankind.

This wisdom is just as applicable to our financial lives as it is to anything else. The things that we worry about, the drama that we cause ourselves and the attachments that our minds form around money function as if we are in a fixed state always and nothing will ever change. When we worry about a tight budget, we are assuming that our income and expenditure will be fixed for eternity. When we hoard too much money out of fear, we are ignoring the fact that we are certainly going to die and that we will part with it anyway. When we avoid investment risk out of attachment to certainty or financial comfort, we are ignoring the fact that, fundamentally, nothing is truly safe or constant.

You don't even need to look back through history to appreciate this perspective. Look at the world around you right now. We are living at a time of exponential technological change. Artificial intelligence and quantum computing promise to challenge the very structures of our society. With computing set to outperform human abilities at some point in the future, our relationships with money, wealth, scarcity and resources may completely change (if they haven't already by the time you are reading this). Medical innovations and breakthroughs could mean that life expectancy significantly increases and, as a result, the way we think about or use money could alter dramatically. On the other hand, the risk of health catastrophes such as pandemics cannot be ruled out either. Markets will crash again at some point; interest rates will change; new political movements and governments will come and go; and the banking system will face challenges. When these things will happen is anyone's guess; but if history is anything to go by, the world (and indeed, the universe as a whole) is inherently full of uncertainty. Everything is impermanent and will continually evolve. Just like your thinking. So, don't take your thoughts so seriously when they are trying to negatively trigger you.

What I am trying to outline here is that nothing is certain – and it never will be. Even if we worried about or pondered over every potential eventuality (financial or otherwise), we could never possibly get everything right and we would be robbing ourselves of the present moment.

I have worked with hundreds of individuals and businesses over the years, assisting them with planning their finances, working towards their goals and allocating their money to align with these objectives. One thing I can tell you for certain is that goals change, hardship arises, windfalls and inheritances arrive, loved ones are lost, children grow up, children need financial help, retirement plans evolve, people get divorced and legislation changes – all of which can upend the best financial plans made with the best of intentions. These things all require a change of course; remaining balanced and rational when it comes to your money makes navigating them much more straightforward. Your experiences are the sum of your thoughts. You can decide how you experience such events and changes, and how hard or easy to make them for yourself.

Our financial plans, asset values and life trajectories are all fickle entities. A detached, arm's-length approach can ensure that you make financial decisions logically and are comfortable with altering them when you need to – something which, for most people, will be inevitable no matter how much or how little money they have. Change, at some point, is inevitable. Get comfortable with change and you can get comfortable with money.

Pinning your well-being on something as fickle as money guarantees a roller coaster of money-mind turbulence. Instead, try to remember the reality of how your mind forms experiences and be in control of your tranquillity and your finances simultaneously.

37

Conclusion – a Clear Path Forward

Money is clearly important. To conclude this journey without acknowledging this fact once again would be irresponsible. We need money to function appropriately in the world, to provide options to explore and to allow us to pursue our goals, interests and values. The role of money both in our personal lives and out there in wider society cannot be ignored. Growing wealth, saving for a rainy day, protecting your family from shocks and saving for retirement are all necessary; and treating your finances with respect and due consideration is of great importance to the societal structures we live in.

However, we need to keep our relationship with money in check. Social media, the press and our peers can greatly influence how we view our financial lives. This happens when we falsely believe the outside-in approach to our well-being and outsource it to external factors.

Without understanding the reality of our experiences, we can allow our minds to form unnecessary attachments that let our egos or emotional minds do the decision-making. This is good for neither our well-being nor our money.

We have explored the things we tell ourselves about what we *say* we want and what we truly *want* when we strip it all back. All we want is to be okay. We have explored the mind and how we create experiences – that is, that our attitudes around money and our experiences with it are entirely generated by ourselves and not by the money itself. This is a simple truth that may feel abstract or contrary to your former understanding, but it is true. We simply take in information and our minds decide how we feel about, react to and interpret that information. This is supported by the undeniable fact that we all experience things differently even if, on the face of it, the circumstances seem the same. The money, the world and the financial decisions that you face are not good, problematic, stressful, upsetting or exciting in themselves. They just *are.* Your own mind decides how you experience them. You *do* have some control over that.

Fundamentally, we do this to ourselves based on the sum of all our previous experiences. Our minds are very powerful tools and we can use them well or we can use them poorly. My whole argument within this book is that a position of mental freedom, clarity and rationality when making financial decisions leads to optimal outcomes. It allows us to use our powerful minds in a better way to make the most of any financial situation, whether we have plenty of resources or not enough. The emotional mind or ego is not the place to access in this domain.

In this book, I have used money as a way of exploring this truth. I have extensive experience in the financial world, helping people with their money, but I am just another traveller on the bigger journey of life.

Of course, you may have gathered by this point that the advantages of this fundamental understanding about how the mind creates experiences extend far beyond money alone. We can apply it to other aspects of our lives just as easily and the benefits will be just as profound.

To help bring this concept to life and make it more tangible, we have also explored some wisdom from multiple disciplines, such as Western philosophy, Buddhism, Stoicism, Christianity and other ancient teachings from around the world. The reason some of these teachings still resonate so deeply today and have prevailed throughout many cultures and historical epochs is because they address the true human experience, not the stories we often tell ourselves. When we are caught up with money or the wider obstacles of the world out there, it is easy to forget this truth.

In an attempt to substantiate these deeper forms of inquiry, I have used real-world examples of people I have worked with and their financial experiences when making decisions on debt, investing, approaching risk, setting budgets and other matters that you may experience yourself from time to time. These examples show how the feeling-generated experiences that we often have can cause us to make overly restrictive decisions or, conversely, unnecessarily reckless decisions. It also shows how a simple change of thought can give rise to a completely different experience.

Clarity, detachment and balance are the answer to ensuring that we give ourselves the best life experiences we can, while not suffering in the process. Hopefully, some of the different ways to approach decision-making that we have explored together in these chapters will help you to develop a new relationship with your money in the future.

Without embracing this need for clarity, it is hard to build your financial knowledge and produce optimal outcomes in a way that aligns with what you truly want your money to do for you. You are not money's servant; money is *your* servant. Make use of it in the way that helps you to live a fruitful life both now and in the future.

This is *your* journey.

This isn't something that you will suddenly be perfect at every time. I still get caught up in the mind frenzy about money myself – often! But the joy in this new-found understanding is that it's an ongoing endeavour. It is something that you can spot more quickly when you are in the right headspace. And when you notice it, you can remind yourself of the reality of the experience and let it pass, then approach things again from a more considered position. This will help to create some much-needed space between you and your financial situation while still treating it with the respect it deserves.

It would be completely understandable if, having finished this book with a much better intellectual understanding of your mind's workings and its relationship with money, you still find yourself yearning for the 'how'. I get it. I have done my best to provide you with some potentially helpful questions to ask yourself when confronted with everyday financial decisions. In truth, however, there isn't really much else to know, other than committing yourself to observing your own thoughts without judgement. The more you do this, the more you will see the mind in a new way – as a partner rather than your whole nature – and ultimately, the more power you will give yourself to take control of how it operates. Meditation is extremely helpful in this regard; as is allocating time for mental training in the same way you would for exercising your physical body. Explore different ways of doing this and you will find what works for you.

There are no tools or intellectual applications required, other than the willingness and dedication to see it for yourself. When you spend time in observation, you will eventually discover that there is a perfectly still and considered part of you that is doing this observing. This is your pure conscious state – your awareness. By returning to this place when faced with financial decisions, you can have confidence that the decision you make, in that given moment, is not borne out of attachment or emotional responses. This doesn't mean that every financial decision that you make will be the right one; but you can take comfort in the fact that these decisions will be more true to yourself and not conjured up on a whim.

The compound benefits over time can help you to shape a financial life that is much more aligned with who you are. It may lead to new business ventures, creative projects, acceptance of a risk, avoidance of a risk, a new savings plan or a new way of life. It may help you to realise that you had what you wanted all along. Only you can ever know what is true to you.

Now that you have this new understanding and have explored the money-mind relationship and applied it to your own situation, you will be able to begin examining the more practical elements of your personal finances. Take some time to reflect and you can then consult the vast swathe of resources available. There are many 'how to' books out there from seasoned professionals providing insights and tips on financial products, planning, tax efficiency and monetary growth. You may also wish to seek assistance from a suitably qualified professional to help you navigate the complexities of the financial world if you don't have the confidence or inclination to do this yourself. There are plenty of good advisers out there.

Whether you're feeling trapped, grieving a loss, navigating divorce, dealing with an estate, stuck in a cycle of spending or simply not enjoying the life you've built, remember: the mind is where you look first for change. Soften your attachments and there will be more room for fresh and productive thinking.

Spiritual growth isn't some abstract or religious pursuit. It simply involves observing your true inner space. With observation comes awareness – and with awareness come power and freedom. This is where your new financial life begins.

I used to hate queues. Now I enjoy them. The idea for this book came during a 20-minute meditation. I healed old wounds. My marriage got better. I listened more. I found parenting easier. I started to listen to the birds twittering outside the window. I stopped needing to prove myself. I started doing more meaningful work. My relationship with money relaxed but grew in respect. And strangely – rather beautifully – my financial world improved, and I now get more done.

It wasn't a quick fix and it has been far from perfect. But it completely changed my life. This work is subtle, but it's profound. I implore you to sit with it. Spend time with yourself. Listen inward. Hopefully, it will do the same for you.

The objective of this book was never to tell you what to buy, what to do or which financial strategies to employ. The aim was rather to help you create enough space to approach your next steps or consider your current position with focus, clarity and freedom. Find your 'why'; the 'how' we will look at next time.

As countless great thinkers have taught us, peace and fulfilment lie within. Money gives us options – and this is a great thing to pursue and work on – but the notion of freedom is an internal pursuit. Financial freedom is not about having no commitments or obligations; it's about being free of internal financial insecurity. You have had the capacity for that all along.

Enjoy the ride.

Acknowledgements

To Sophie, Arthur and Arabella. You are my world and this is for you. I love you with every fibre of my being.

I would also like to express my gratitude to Jonathan Armes as a contributor to this project. Your original work with me helped me to open up my consciousness, triggering a long period of reflection and self-inquiry which ultimately led to this book. The work we did together planning this important message was instrumental and I can't thank you enough.

About the Author

ADAM COCKERHAM IS a Chartered Financial Planner, a Fellow of the Personal Finance Society and corporate director of a financial advice and wealth management firm, which currently has over £200 million under management. Adam advises businesses, entrepreneurs, families, senior public figures, politicians and C-suite executives of FTSE 100 companies, as well as the general public. Adam also holds a master's degree in applied economics, during which he studied behavioural insights into financial decision-making and neurofinance. He is also a partner of The Openwork Partnership and is a leading financial planner within one of the UK's largest financial advice networks.

Adam's opinion pieces have been published by the *Financial Times Adviser* and he has previously operated a small speechwriting business for executives of large multinational companies, academics and other speakers at high-profile events.

He takes a keen interest in philosophy and spiritual teachings and enjoys looking at the bigger questions of our existence.